Sunday Night Suppers

Barbara C. Jones

Cookbook Resources LLC, Highland Village, Texas

Sunday Night Suppers

1st Printing October 2006

ISBN 9781931294799
Library of Congress Number: 2006930533

Illustrations by Nancy Griffith

Edited, Designed, Published and Manufactured
in the United States of America

Cookbook Resources, LLC
541 Doubletree Drive
Highland Village, Texas 75077
Toll free 866-229-2665
www.cookbookresources.com

Bringing Families To The Table

Introduction

Somehow Sunday nights are just different. There are no PTA meetings, no soccer games, no practices and no big dates (usually). They are "stay-at-home" nights, "wind-down-from-the-weekend" nights and "get-ready-for-the-week" nights. Sunday nights are perfect for something special, not necessarily big or fancy, but just something that's a little different, a little out of the ordinary.

Maybe you pick one night every week when everyone must be at home to sit around the kitchen table, have supper together and get re-acquainted. Sunday night is a good night.

Maybe you pick one night once a month when the kids do the cooking. You want to start them early for the day they're on their own. You practice with them now and you won't have to worry that they are hungry when they're in their first apartment.

Maybe you pick one night every month or one night every week during the school year when you have soup. That's right…SOUP. Maybe Sunday night becomes soup night!

Or, maybe one night every week, Dad cooks supper. Since he makes lots of rules, maybe he'll break a few of them and decide that you can have breakfast at night. Bacon and egg specials, waffles, pancakes and who knows what else, all on Sunday night. Maybe, he even breaks the "eat healthy" rule and everyone makes his own super-duper, triple scooper, cherry-on-top banana splits. Maybe…

Maybe the little things are more important than we realize. Maybe these little things are really big things we never forget. And maybe, these little things are family traditions that make the bonds stronger and the memories more vivid.

Families who gather at the table for regular family meals are stronger and better for the experience and food they share. We hope you find some ideas for your own family traditions in *Sunday Night Suppers*. We hope you recognize the importance of sharing time and meals together. If you do, our families will be stronger, our nation will be stronger and our own little part of the world will feel a little safer and a little more loving.

Contents

APPETIZER SUPPERS

Wings and Strips

Raspberry-Glazed Chicken Wings

¾ cup seedless raspberry jam	180 ml
¼ cup cider vinegar	60 ml
¼ cup soy sauce	60 ml
1 teaspoon garlic powder	5 ml
16 whole chicken wings	

- In saucepan, combine jam, vinegar, soy sauce, garlic powder and 1 teaspoon (5 ml) pepper. Bring to a boil and boil 1 minute.
- Cut chicken wings into 3 sections and discard wing tips. Place wings in large bowl, add raspberry mixture and toss to coat. Cover and refrigerate for 4 hours.
- Line 10 x 15-inch (25 x 38 cm) baking pan with foil and grease foil. Use slotted spoon to place wings in pan and reserve marinade.
- Bake at 350° (176° C) for 30 minutes and turn once. Cook reserved marinade for 10 minutes, brush over wings and bake 25 minutes longer.

■

Cheese Strips

1 loaf thin-sliced bread	
1 (8 ounce) package shredded cheddar cheese	227 g
6 slices bacon, fried, drained, coarsely broken	
½ cup chopped onion	120 ml
1 cup mayonnaise	240 ml

- Remove crust from bread. Combine cheese, bacon, onion and mayonnaise and spread filling over slices. Cut into 3 strips and place on cookie sheet.
- Bake at 400° (204° C) for 10 minutes. For a special touch, add ⅓ cup (80 ml) slivered almonds, toasted.

Finger Sandwich Pick-Ups

Peanut-Butter Spread

1 (8 ounce) package cream cheese, softened	227 g
1⅔ cups creamy peanut butter	400 ml
½ cup powdered sugar	120 ml
1 tablespoon milk	15 ml

- In mixer, cream all ingredients. Serve spread with apple wedges or graham crackers.

■

Beef or Ham Spread

1 pound leftover roast beef or ham	.5 kg
¾ cup sweet pickle relish	180 ml
½ onion, finely diced	
2 celery ribs, chopped	
2 hard-boiled eggs, chopped	
Mayonnaise	

- Chop meat in food processor and add relish, onion, celery and eggs. Add a little salt and pepper. Fold in enough mayonnaise to make mixture spread easily and chill. Spread on crackers or bread for sandwiches.

■

Green-Olive Spread

1 (8 ounce) package cream cheese, softened	227 g
⅔ cup mayonnaise	160 ml
¾ cup chopped pecans	180 ml
1 cup green olives, drained, chopped	240 ml

- In mixing bowl, blend cream cheese and mayonnaise until smooth. Add remaining ingredients and ¼ teaspoon (1 ml) pepper, mix well and refrigerate. Serve on crackers or make sandwiches with party rye bread.

■ ■ ■

Dancing Wings

Dancing Honey Wings

1½ cups flour	360 ml
¼ cup (½ stick) butter	60 ml
18 - 20 chicken drummettes and wings	
¾ cup honey	80 ml
⅔ cup chili sauce	160 ml

- Preheat oven to 325° (162 C). Combine flour and a little salt in shallow bowl and dredge chicken in flour. Melt butter in large skillet and brown wings a few at a time on medium heat. Place in sprayed 9 x 13-inch (23 x 33 cm) baking pan.
- In small bowl, combine honey and chili sauce, mix well and pour over each wing to make them dance. Cover and bake for 45 minutes.

■

Stuffed Jalapenos

12 - 15 medium jalapeno chilies with stems	
1 (8 ounce) package cream cheese, softened	227 g
¾ cup finely shredded Montery Jack cheese	180 ml
3 slices cooked ham, finely chopped	
1 tablespoon lime juice	15 ml
1 tablespoon garlic powder	15 ml

- Preheat oven to 325° (162 C). Cut each jalapeno lengthwise through steam and remove ribs and seeds. (Use rubber gloves.)
- In bowl, combine remaining ingredients and mix well. Fill each jalapeno half with cheese mixture. Place on sprayed baking sheet and bake for 15 minutes. Cool, slightly before serving.

■ ■ ■

Italian Spread

Tex-Mex Pizzas

8 flour tortillas	
1 (8 ounce) carton marinara sauce	227 g
1 (15 ounce) can bean dip	425 g
1 (8 ounce) can whole kernel corn, drained	227 g
1 (8 ounce) package shredded Mexican 4-cheese blend	227 g

- Preheat oven to 425° (220° C). Place tortillas on 2 foil-lined sprayed baking sheets. Bake about 4 minutes on each side or until crisp and light brown.
- In bowl, combine marinara sauce and bean dip and mix well. Spread mixture on each tortilla and sprinkle with corn and cheese. Bake another 3 minutes or until cheese melts. Cut each tortilla in half to serve.

■

Sweet Cheese Garlic Spread

2 (8 ounce) packages cream cheese, softened	2 (227 g)
¼ cup apricot preserves	60 ml
1 teaspoon minced garlic	5 ml
¼ cup finely chopped walnuts	60 ml
3 fresh green onions tops only, finely chopped	

- In mixing bowl, beat cream cheese and preserves until they blend well. Stir in garlic, walnuts and onions and chill. Serve with assorted crackers.

■ ■ ■

Holy Guacamoly

Jack Quesadillas

¼ cup ricotta cheese, divided	60 ml
6 (6-inch) corn tortillas	6 (15 cm)
⅔ cup shredded Monterey Jack cheese	160 ml
1 (4 ounce) can diced green chilies, drained	114 g

- Spread 1 tablespoon (15 ml) ricotta over tortilla. Add 1 heaping tablespoon (15 ml) cheese and 1 tablespoon (15 ml) chilies. Place second tortilla on top. Repeat to make 2 more quesadillas.
- In heated skillet, add 1 quesadilla and cook for 3 minutes on each side. Remove from heat and cut into 4 wedges. Repeat with remaining quesadillas. Serve warm with salsa.

■

Holy Guacamoly

4 avocados, peeled	
½ cup salsa	120 ml
¼ cup sour cream	60 ml

- Split avocados and remove seeds. Mash avocado with fork. Add salsa, sour cream and 1 teaspoon (5 ml) salt. Serve with tortilla chips.

■

Chili-Cheese Balls

1 (8 ounce) package grated sharp cheddar cheese, softened	227 g
½ cup (1 stick) butter, softened	120 ml
1 cup flour	240 ml
1 (4 ounce) can chopped green chilies	114 g

- Mix cheese and butter. Add flour, green chilies and ½ teaspoon (2 ml) salt. Form dough into 2-inch (5 cm) balls and place on cookie sheet. Bake at 375° (190° C) for 14 to 15 minutes.

■ ■ ■

A Good Catch

Garlic Shrimp

1 clove garlic, minced	
⅔ cup chili sauce	160 ml
½ pound thin bacon strips	227 g
1 pound medium shrimp, cooked	.5 kg

- Add garlic to chili sauce and set aside for several hours. Broil bacon on 1 side only. Cut in half.
- Dip shrimp in chili sauce and wrap with ½ bacon strip on uncooked side out; fasten with toothpicks. Refrigerate. Just before serving, broil shrimp until bacon is crisp.

■

Oyster Bites

1 (5 ounce) can smoked oysters, drained, chopped	143g
⅔ cup herb-seasoned stuffing mix	160 ml
8 slices bacon, halved, partially cooked	

- Combine oysters, stuffing mix and ¼ cup (60 ml) water. Add 1 teaspoon (5 ml) water if mixture seems too dry.
- Form into balls and use 1 tablespoon (15 ml) mixture for each. Wrap ½ slice bacon around each and secure with toothpick. Place on rack in shallow baking pan. Cook at 350° (176° C) for 25 to 30 minutes.

■

Toasted Crab

¾ cup shredded cheddar cheese	180 ml
½ cup (1 stick) butter, softened	120 ml
1 (6 ounce) can crabmeat, drained, flaked	168 g
6 English muffins, halved	

- In bowl, combine cheese, softened butter and crabmeat and mix well. Spread mixture on each muffin half. Cut each muffin into quarters and place on baking sheet. Broil for 5 minutes and serve hot.

■ ■ ■

Dippidy-Do-Da

Believe it or not, you get meat and veggies with this "dippy" supper.

Unbelievable Crab Dip

1 (16 ounce) package cubed processed cheese	.5 kg
2 (6.5 ounce) cans crabmeat, drained, flaked	2 (175 g)
1 bunch fresh green onions with tops, chopped	
2 cups mayonnaise	480 ml

• Melt cheese in top of double boiler. Add remaining ingredients and ½ teaspoon (2 ml) salt. Serve hot or at room temperature with assorted crackers.

■

Broccoli-Cheese Dip

1 (10 ounce) can broccoli-cheese soup	280 g
1 (10 ounce) package frozen, chopped broccoli, thawed	280 g
½ cup sour cream	120 ml
2 teaspoons of dijon-style mustard	10 ml

• In saucepan, combine soup, broccoli, sour cream, ½ teaspoon (2 ml) salt and mustard and mix well. Heat and serve hot.

■

Confetti Dip

1 (15 ounce) can whole kernel corn, drained	425 g
1 (15 ounce) can kidney or pinto beans, drained	425 g
⅓ cup Italian salad dressing	80 ml
1 (16 ounce) jar salsa	.5 kg

• Combine all ingredients. Refrigerate several hours before serving. Serve with chips.

■

(Continued on next page.)

Dippidy-Do-Da

(Continued)

Spinach-Artichoke Dip

2 (10 ounce) boxes frozen spinach, thawed, drained	2 (280 g)
1 (14 ounce) jar marinated artichoke hearts, drained, finely chopped	396 g
1 cup mayonnaise	240 ml
2 cups shredded mozzarella cheese	480 ml

- Drain spinach well with several layers of paper towels.
- Combine, spinach, artichoke hearts, mayonnaise and cheese and mix well.
- Cover and refrigerate. Serve with chips.

■

Black Bean Salsa

1 (15 ounce) can black beans, drained	425 g
4 - 6 green onions with tops, diced	
½ - ¾ cup snipped fresh cilantro leaves	120 ml
1 - 2 cloves garlic, minced	
1 tablespoon oil	15 ml
1 teaspoon fresh lime juice	5 ml

- Mix all ingredients and chill before serving.

■ ■ ■

Jose's Choice

Hot Sombrero Dip

2 (15 ounce) cans bean dip	2 (425 g)
1 pound lean ground beef, browned, cooked	.5 kg
1 (4 ounce) can green chilies	114 g
1 cup hot salsa	240 ml
1½ cups shredded cheddar cheese	360 ml

- Layer bean dip, ground beef, chilies and salsa in 3-quart (3 L) baking dish. Top with cheese.
- Bake at 350° (176° C) just until cheese melts, about 10 or 15 minutes.
- Serve with tortilla chips.

■

Quick-Draw Salsa

4 tomatoes, chopped	
4 green onions with tops, chopped	
1 (7 ounce) can chopped green chilies	198 g

- Combine all ingredients with salt and pepper to taste and serve with chips or tortillas.

■ ■ ■

Here's Lookin' At Ya'

Elegant Crab Dip

1 (6.5 ounce) can white crabmeat, drained	175 g
1 (8 ounce) package cream cheese	227 g
½ cup (1 stick) butter	120 ml

- In saucepan, combine crabmeat, cream cheese and butter, heat and mix thoroughly. Transfer to hot chafing dish and serve with chips.

■

Crunchy Bread Sticks

1 package hot dog buns	
1 cup (2 sticks) butter, melted	240 ml
Garlic powder	
Parmesan cheese	

- Preheat oven to 225° (107° C). Take each half bun and slice in half lengthwise. Use a pastry brush to butter all bread sticks and sprinkle a light amount of garlic powder and just a few sprinkles of paprika and parmesan cheese. Place on cookie sheet and bake for about 45 minutes.

■

Green Eyes

4 large dill pickles
4 slices boiled ham
Light cream cheese
Garlic powder

- Dry pickles with paper towels and set aside. Lightly coat one side of ham slices with cream cheese and sprinkle a little pepper and a little garlic powder on each slice.
- Roll pickle in slice of ham coated with cream cheese mixture, chill and cut into circles.

■ ■ ■

Dippy Party Night

Party Sausages

1 cup ketchup	240 ml
1 cup plum jelly	240 ml
1 tablespoon lemon juice	15 ml
2 tablespoons prepared mustard	30 ml
2 (5 ounce) packages tiny smoked sausages	2 (143 g)

- In saucepan, combine all ingredients except sausages, heat and mix well. Add sausages and simmer for 10 minutes. Serve with cocktail toothpicks.

Easy Tuna Dip

1 (6 ounce) can tuna, drained	168 g
1 (1 ounce) package Italian salad dressing mix	28 g
1 (8 ounce) carton sour cream	227 g
2 green onions with tops, chopped	

- Combine all ingredients and mix well. Let rest several hours before serving.

Ambrosia Spread

1 (11 ounce) can mandarin orange sections, drained	312 g
1 (8 ounce) carton cream cheese with pineapple, softened	227 g
¼ cup flaked coconut	60 ml
¼ cup slivered almonds, chopped	60 ml

- Chop orange sections and set aside. Whip cream cheese and fold in coconut and almonds. Spread on date-nut bread, banana bread, etc.

Squares At The Table

Cheesy Vegetable Squares

1 (8 ounce) package refrigerated crescent rolls	227 g
1 (8 ounce) package cream cheese, softened	227 g
½ cup mayonnaise	120 ml
1 (1 ounce) package ranch-style dressing mix	28 g
1 cup broccoli slaw	240 ml
1½ cups shredded cheddar cheese	360 ml

- Preheat oven to 350° (176° C). Press crescent roll dough in 9 x 13-inch baking dish and press perforations together to seal. Bake 12 minutes or until dough is golden brown and cool.

- With mixer, beat cream cheese, mayonnaise and dressing mix. Spread over crust. Sprinkle slaw over crust and top with cheese. Gently press into cream cheese mixture. Cover and chill at least 3 hours. Cut into squares to serve.

■

Extra Special Queso

1 pound lean ground beef	.5 kg
1 (15 ounce) jar medium salsa con queso	425 g
1 (16 ounce) jar salsa	.5 kg
1 (15 ounce) can black beans, rinsed, drained	425 g

- In skillet, cook meat over medium heat and stir in remaining ingredients. Bring to a boil and stir constantly. Reduce heat to low and simmer for 5 minutes. Serve with tortilla scoops.

■ ■ ■

Nibbling Vaqueros

Cheesy Quick Broccoli Quesadillas

1 (8 ounce) package shredded cheddar cheese	227 g
1 (10 ounce) package frozen chopped broccoli, drained	280 g
⅓ cup salsa	80 ml
8 (6-inch) flour tortillas	8 (15 cm)

- In bowl combine cheese, broccoli and salsa and mix well. Spoon about ¼ cup (60 ml) cheese-broccoli mixture onto 1 side of each tortilla and fold tortilla over filling.
- Place 2 quesadillas at a time in large sprayed skillet. Cook over medium meat about 3 minutes on both sides or until tortillas are light brown. Repeat for remaining quesadillas.

■

Hot Artichoke Dip

1 (14 ounce) can artichoke hearts, drained, chopped	396 g
1 cup mayonnaise	240 ml
1 cup grated parmesan cheese	240 ml

- Preheat oven to 350° (176° C). Combine all ingredients and place in sprayed 8-inch (20 cm) pie plate. Bake for 25 minutes.

■

Sweet Nibblers

1 (6 ounce) package semi-sweet chocolate chips	168 g
1 cup chopped peanuts	240 ml
7 cups Crispix cereal	1.6 L
1½ cups powdered sugar	360 ml

- In heavy sauce pan, melt chocolate over low heat and stir constantly. Stir peanuts and cereal and stir until it coats evenly. Place powdered sugar in large baggie, add cereal and close bag. Toss cereal gently until it coasts evenly; chill.

■ ■ ■

Circus Rides

Spinach Pinwheels

1 (8 ounce) can crescent dinner rolls	227 g
1 (8 ounce) package garlic-herb cream cheese	
softened	227 g
6 thin slices cooked ham	
30 fresh spinach leaves, stems removed	

- Preheat oven to 350° (176° C). Separate crescent dough into 4 rectangles and press perforations together to seal. Generously spread rectangles with cheese and leave ¼-inch (.6 cm) around edge with cheese. Top with ham and spinach.

- Start at short side of dough, roll each rectangle and press edges to seal. Chill for 30 minutes to 1 hour and slice each roll into 6 slices. Place on baking sheet and bake about 15 minutes.

■

Creamy Sausage Dip

1 (16 ounce) roll sausage	.5 kg
2 (8 ounce) packages cream cheese	2 (227 g)
1 (10 ounce) can tomatoes and green chilies	280 g

- In skillet brown sausage over medium heat; drain. Add remaining ingredients and stir until cream cheese melts.

■

Quick Need-A-Snack-Fix Nachos

Large tortilla chips	
1 (15 ounce) can refried beans	425 g
1 (8 ounce) package cheddar cheese	227 g
1 (16 ounce) jar chunky salsa	.5 kg

- Spread tortilla chips on microwave-safe plate. Top each chip with dab of refried beans and sprinkle of cheese. Top with heaping teaspoon (5 ml) of salsa. Microwave on high just until cheese melts.

■ ■ ■

Nutty Kind Of Meal

Puffy Taco Shells

½ pound pork sausage, cooked, crumbled	227 g
1 (8 ounce) package shredded cheddar cheese	227 g
⅓ cup mild taco sauce	80 ml
1½ cups baking mix	360 ml

- Preheat oven to 375° (190° C). In mixing bowl, combine all ingredients and mix well. Form into 1-inch (2.5 cm) balls and place on baking sheet. Bake about 18 minutes or until balls are light brown.

■

Cucumber Dip

2 seedless cucumbers, shredded, well drained	
1 (8 ounce) carton sour cream	227 g
2 teaspoons white vinegar	10 ml
2 teaspoons olive oil	10 ml
1 teaspoon minced garlic	5 ml

- Combine all ingredients with 1 teaspoon (5 ml) salt and mix well. Chill and serve with wheat crackers or pita wedges.

■

Barbecued Walnuts*

3 tablespoons butter, melted	45 ml
¼ cup Worcestershire sauce	60 ml
2 tablespoons ketchup	30 ml
5 cups walnut halves	1.3 L

- Preheat oven to 400° (204° C). In bowl combine butter, Worcestershire sauce, ketchup and dash of salt and mix well. Pour over walnuts and stir until they coat well. Spoon into 9 x 13-inch (23 x 33 cm) baking pan; bake for 20 minutes and stir every 5 minutes. Remove from oven and pour onto 2 layers of paper towels. Cool before serving.

■ ■ ■

SOUPS, SALADS &
SANDWICHES

You're Kidding Soup

Quick and Easy Peanut Soup

¼ cup (½ stick) butter	60 ml
1 onion, finely chopped	
2 ribs celery, chopped	
2 (10 ounce) cans cream of chicken soup	2 (280 g)
2 soup cans milk	
1¼ cups crunchy-style peanut butter	300 ml

- Melt butter in saucepan and saute onion and celery over low heat. Blend in soup and milk and stir. Add peanut butter and continue to heat until mixture blends well.

■

Broccoli-Noodle Salad

1 cup slivered almonds, toasted	240 ml
1 cup sunflower seeds, toasted	240 ml
2 (3 ounce) packages chicken-flavored ramen noodles	2 (84 g)
1 (16 ounce) package broccoli slaw	.5 kg
1 (8 ounce) bottle Italian salad dressing	227 g

- Toast almonds and sunflower seeds in oven at 275° (135° C) for about 10 minutes.
- Break up ramen noodles and mix with slaw, almonds and sunflower seeds.
- Toss with Italian salad dressing and chill.

Way Down South

Ham and Fresh Okra Soup

1 ham hock bone	
1 cup frozen butter beans or lima beans	240 ml
1½ pounds chicken or ham, cooked, cubed	.7 kg
1 (15 ounce) can chopped, stewed tomatoes	425 g
3 cups small, whole okra	710 ml
2 large onions, diced	

- Boil ham hock in 1½ quarts (1.5 L) water for about 1 hour, 30 minutes. Add remaining ingredients and salt and pepper to taste. Boil for 1 more hour. Serve over rice.

■

Nutty Green Salad

6 cups torn, mixed salad greens	1.5 L
1 medium zucchini, sliced	
1 (8 ounce) can sliced water chestnuts, drained	227 g
½ cup peanuts	120 ml
⅓ cup Italian salad dressing	80 ml

- Toss greens, zucchini, water chestnuts and peanuts.
- When ready to serve, add salad dressing and toss.

■ ■ ■

Unbelievable Soup Night

EDITORS
CHOICE

Incredible Broccoli-Cheese Soup

1 (10 ounce) box frozen chopped broccoli	280 g
3 tablespoons butter	45 ml
½ onion, finely chopped	
¼ cup flour	60 ml
1 (16 ounce) carton half-and-half cream	.5 kg
1 (14 ounce) can chicken broth	396 g
½ teaspoon summer savory	2 ml
1 (16 ounce) package cubed, mild Mexican processed cheese	.5 kg

- Punch several holes in box of broccoli and microwave on high 5 minutes. Rotate box in microwave and cook on high another 4 minutes. Leave in microwave for 3 minutes.
- In large saucepan, melt butter and cook onion until it is translucent. Add flour, stir and gradually add half-and-half, chicken broth, ½ teaspoon (2 ml) salt, ¼ teaspoon (1 ml) pepper and summer savory and stir constantly.
- Heat until mixture thickens. (Do not boil.) Add cheese and stir constantly until cheese melts. Add cooked broccoli and serve hot.

■

Spicy Cornbread Twists

3 tablespoons (⅓ stick) butter	45 ml
½ cup cornmeal	120 ml
¼ teaspoon cayenne pepper	1 ml
1 (11 ounce) can refrigerated soft breadsticks	312 g

- Preheat oven to 350° (176° C). Place butter in pie plate and melt butter in oven. Remove from oven as soon as butter melts. On wax paper, mix cornmeal and cayenne pepper.
- Roll breadsticks in butter and in cornmeal mixture. Twist breadsticks according to label directions and place on large cookie sheet. Bake for 15 to 18 minutes.

■ ■ ■

Farmhouse Special

Slow-Cook Navy Bean and Ham Soup

1½ cups dry navy beans	360 ml
1 carrot, finely chopped	
¼ cup celery, finely chopped	60 ml
1 small onion, finely chopped	
1 (¾ pound) ham hock	340 g

- Soak beans for 8 to 12 hours and drain. Place all ingredients with 5 cups (1.3 L) water, ½ teaspoon (2 ml) salt and a dash of pepper in 2-quart slow cooker. Cook for 8 to 10 hours on LOW setting.
- Remove ham hock and discard skin, fat and bone. Cut meat in small pieces and place in soup. Beans can be mashed if desired.

■

Spinach-Apple Salad

1 (10 ounce) package fresh spinach	280 g
⅓ cup frozen orange juice concentrate, thawed	80 ml
¾ cup mayonnaise	180 ml
1 red apple with peel, diced	
5 slices bacon, fried, crumbled	

- Tear spinach into small pieces. Mix orange juice concentrate and mayonnaise.
- When ready to serve, peel, chop apple and mix with spinach. Pour orange juice-mayonnaise mixture over salad and top with bacon.

Ridin' The Trail

This is a real country supper: beans and cornbread.

Trail Drive Whistlers

2 pounds dried pinto beans	1 kg
1 medium piece salt pork	
5 slices uncooked bacon, chopped	
2 (10 ounce) cans tomatoes and green chilies	2 (280 g)
1 onion, chopped	
½ teaspoon ground cumin	2 ml
2 teaspoons minced garlic	10 ml

- Place pinto beans in large saucepan. Rinse and cover with water. Soak overnight or at least 3 hours. Drain and cover with fresh water.
- Add salt pork, bacon, tomatoes, green chilies and onion. Bring to boil, add more water if needed, lower heat and simmer for 3 hours or until beans are tender.
- Add cumin, garlic and ½ teaspoon (2 ml) salt in the last 30 minutes of cooking.

TIP: *These beans will be good even if you leave out the green chilies and cumin.*

■

Cheddar Cornbread

2 (8.5 ounce) packages cornbread-muffin mix	2 (240 g)
2 eggs, beaten	
1 cup plain yogurt	240 ml
1 (14 ounce) can cream-style corn	396 g
½ cup shredded cheddar cheese	120 ml

- Combine cornbread mix, eggs and yogurt in bowl and blend well. Stir in corn and cheese.
- Pour into greased 9 x 13-inch (23 x 33 cm) baking dish. Bake at 400° (204° C) for 18 to 20 minutes or until light brown.

■ ■ ■

Old-Fashioned Remedy

Old-Fashioned Chicken-Noodle Soup

1 (3 - 4 pound) whole chicken	1.3 kg
1 carrot, chopped	
2 ribs celery with leaves, chopped	
½ - ¾ cup egg noodles, cooked	120 ml

- Wash whole chicken and giblets and put in large soup pot. Add 7 to 8 cups (1.6 L) water, carrot and celery and bring to boil. Reduce heat and simmer, partially covered, for 45 minutes to 1 hour or until meat is tender.
- Remove chicken from soup pot and cool. Continue simmering and spoon off fat from top of liquid when needed.
- Bone chicken and put all bones and skin back into soup pot. Continue to simmer for 3 to 4 hours. Turn heat off and strain chicken stock in large bowl. Add chopped chicken and cooked egg noodles. Salt and pepper to taste.

■

Gingerbread Muffins

1 (18 ounce) box gingerbread mix	510 g
1 egg	
2 (1.5 ounce) boxes seedless raisins	2 (45 g)

- Combine gingerbread mix, 1¼ cups (300 ml) water and egg and mix well. Stir in raisins and pour into greased muffin tins half full.
- Bake at 350° (176° C) for 20 minutes or until toothpick comes out clean.

Couch Potato Soup

Easy Potato Soup

1 (16 ounce) package frozen hash brown potatoes	.5 kg
1 cup chopped onion	240 ml
1 (14 ounce) can chicken broth	396 g
1 (10 ounce) can fiesta-nacho soup	280 g
1 (10 ounce) can cream of chicken soup	280 g
2 cups milk	480 ml

- Combine potatoes, onion and 2 cups (480 ml) water in large saucepan and bring to boil. Cover, reduce heat and simmer 30 minutes. Stir in broth, soups and milk and heat thoroughly.

■

Texas Beer Bread

3 cups self-rising flour	710 ml
¼ cup sugar	60 ml
1 (12 ounce) can beer, room temperature	340 g
1 egg, beaten	
2 tablespoons butter, melted	30 ml

- Preheat oven to 350° (176° C). In bowl, combine flour, sugar and beer; just mix until it blends well. Spoon into 9 x 3-inch (23 x 8 cm) loaf pan.
- To give bread a nice glaze, combine egg and 1 tablespoon (15 ml) water; brush top of loaf with mixture.
- Bake for 40 to 45 minutes; when removing loaf from oven, brush top with melted butter.

Cajun Joy

Cajun Bean Soup

1 (20 ounce) package Cajun-flavored, 16-bean soup mix with flavor packet	567 g
2 cups finely chopped, cooked ham	480 ml
1 chopped onion	
2 (15 ounce) cans stewed tomatoes	2 (425 g)

- Soak beans overnight in large slow cooker. After soaking, drain water and cover with 2 inches (5 cm) water over beans.
- Cover and cook on LOW for 5 to 6 hours or until beans are tender.
- Add ham, onion, stewed tomatoes and flavor packet in bean soup mix. Cook on HIGH for 30 to 45 minutes. Serve with cornbread.

■

Special Rice Salad

1 (6 ounce) package chicken-flavored rice and macaroni	168 g
¾ cup chopped green pepper	180 ml
1 bunch fresh green onion with tops, chopped	
2 (6 ounce) jars marinated artichoke hearts	2 (168 g)
½ - ⅔ cup mayonnaise	120 ml

- Cook rice and macaroni according to package directions (but with no butter), drain and cool.
- Add green pepper, onions, artichoke hearts and mayonnaise, toss and chill.

Close Enough To Pizza

Pizza Soup

3 (10 ounce) cans tomato bisque soup	3 (280 g)
1 (10 ounce) can French onion soup	280 g
2 teaspoons Italian seasoning	10 ml
¾ cup uncooked tiny pasta shells	180 ml
1½ cups shredded mozzarella cheese	360 ml

- In 4 to 6-quart (4 L) slow cooker, place all soup, Italian seasoning and 1½ soup cans water. Turn heat setting to HIGH and cook 1 hour or until mixture is hot.
- Add pasta shells or ditali and cook for 1½ to 2 hours or until pasta is done. Stir several times to keep pasta from sticking to bottom of slow cooker. Turn heat off, add mozzarella cheese and stir until cheese melts.

TIP: *For a special way to serve this soup, sprinkle some french-fried onions over top of each serving.*

■

Fluffy Fruit Salad

2 (20 ounce) cans pineapple tidbits, drained	2 (567 g)
1 (16 ounce) can whole cranberry sauce	.5 kg
2 (11 ounce) cans mandarin oranges, drained	2 (312 g)
½ cup chopped pecans	120 ml
1 (8 ounce) carton whipped topping	227 g

- In bowl, combine pineapple, cranberries, oranges and pecans.
- Fold in whipped topping. Serve in pretty crystal bowl.

Mexican Soup Pot

Chili Soup

3 (15 ounce) cans chili with beans	3 (425 g)
1 (15 ounce) can whole kernel corn, drained	425 g
1 (14 ounce) can beef broth	396 g
2 (15 ounce) cans Mexican stewed tomatoes	2 (425 g)
2 teaspoons ground cumin	10 ml
2 teaspoons chili powder	10 ml

- In 5 to 6-quart (5 to 6 L) slow cooker, combine chili, corn, broth, tomatoes, cumin, chili powder and 1 cup (240 ml) water.
- Cover and cook on LOW for 4 to 5 hours. Serve with warm, buttered flour tortillas.

■

Easy Guacamole Salad

4 avocados, softened	
1 (8 ounce) package cream cheese, softened	227 g
1 (10 ounce) can diced tomatoes and green chilies	280 g
1½ teaspoons garlic salt	7 ml
About 1 tablespoon lemon juice	15 ml

- Peel avocados and mash with fork. In mixing bowl, beat cream cheese until smooth, add avocados and remaining ingredients and mix well.
- Serve on lettuce leaf with a few tortilla chips beside salad.

Cold Winter Night Special

Tasty Black Bean Soup

1 pound hot sausage	.5 kg
1 onion, chopped	
2 (14 ounce) cans chicken broth	2 (396 g)
2 (15 ounce) cans Mexican stewed tomatoes	2 (425 g)
1 green bell pepper, chopped	
2 (15 ounce) cans black beans, rinsed, drained	2 (425 g)

- In large skillet, break up sausage and brown with onion. Drain off fat and place in large slow cooker.
- Add chicken broth, stewed tomatoes, bell pepper, black beans and 1 cup (240 ml) water. Cover and cook on LOW for 3 to 5 hours.

■

Cherry Salad

1 (20 ounce) can cherry pie filling	567 g
1 (20 ounce) can crushed pineapple, drained	567 g
1 (14 ounce) can sweetened condensed milk	396 g
1 cup miniature marshmallows	240 ml
1 cup chopped pecans	240 ml
1 (8 ounce) carton whipped topping	227 g

- In large bowl, combine pie filling, pineapple, condensed milk, marshmallows and pecans. Fold in whipped topping, chill and serve in pretty crystal bowl.

TIP: *You may add a couple drops of red food coloring, if you like a brighter color.*

Soup and Salad Favorite

Chicken and Rice Soup

1 (6 ounce) package long grain, wild rice mix	168 g
1 (1 ounce) envelope chicken-noodle soup mix	28 g
2 (10 ounce) cans cream of chicken soup	2 (280 g)
2 ribs celery, chopped	
1 - 2 cups cooked, cubed chicken	240 ml

- In 5 to 6-quart (5 L) slow cooker, combine rice mix, noodle soup mix, chicken soup, celery, cubed chicken and about 6 cups (1.5 L) water.
- Cover and cook on LOW for 2 to 3 hours.

■

Broccoli-Waldorf Salad

6 cups fresh broccoli florets	1.5 L
1 large red apple with peel, chopped	
½ cup golden raisins	120 ml
½ cup chopped pecans	120 ml
½ cup prepared coleslaw dressing	120 ml

- Combine broccoli, apple, raisins and pecans in large bowl. Drizzle with dressing and toss to coat. Refrigerate. Serve in pretty crystal bowl.

■ ■ ■

Soup and Salad Special

Tasty Turkey Soup

1 (16 ounce) package frozen chopped onions and bell peppers	.5 kg
2 (3 ounce) packages chicken-flavored ramen noodles	2 (84 g)
2 (10 ounce) cans cream of chicken soup	2 (280 g)
1 cup cubed turkey	240 ml

- In soup pot with a little oil, cook onions and peppers just until tender but not brown. Add ramen noodles with seasoning package and 4 cups (1 L) water.
- Cook 5 minutes or until noodles are tender. Stir in chicken soup and turkey. Heat and stir constantly until thoroughly hot.

■

Creamy Fruit Salad

1 (14 ounce) can sweetened condensed milk	396 g
¼ cup lemon juice	60 ml
1 (20 ounce) can peach pie filling	567 g
2 (15 ounce) cans fruit cocktail, drained	2 (425 g)
1 (15 ounce) can pineapple chunks, drained	425 g
1 cup chopped pecans	240 ml
1 (8 ounce) carton whipped topping	227 g

- Combine sweetened condensed milk and lemon juice in large bowl and stir until it mixes well. Add pie filling, fruit cocktail, pineapple and pecans and mix well.
- Fold in whipped topping and stir to blend well. Spoon into bowl, cover and chill several hours before serving.

■ ■ ■

Popeye's Favorite

Quick Spinach-Rice Soup

3 (14 ounce) cans chicken broth	3 (396 g)
2 (12 ounce) packages frozen creamed spinach, thawed	2 (340 g)
1 (10 ounce) can cream of onion soup	280 g
1 (4 ounce) can chopped pimentos	114 g
½ cup instant rice	120 ml

- In soup pot, combine all ingredients plus salt and pepper to taste. Bring to a boil, reduce heat and simmer for 10 minutes.

■

Great Chicken 'N Greens Salad

2 cups skinned, diced rotisserie chicken	480 ml
1 (10 ounce) package mixed greens	280 g
½ chopped sun-dried tomatoes	120 ml
1 red bell pepper, seeded, chopped	
3 tablespoon roasted sunflower seeds	45 ml

Dressing:

½ (8 ounce) bottle vinaigrette salad dressing	½ (227 g)
2 tablespoons refrigerated honey-mustard salad dressing	30 ml

- In salad bowl, combine chicken, greens, tomatoes and bell pepper and toss.
- Combine vinaigrette dressing and honey-mustard dressing, pour over salad and toss. Use more vinaigrette dressing if needed. Sprinkle sunflower seeds over salad and serve.

■ ■ ■

Beans and Barley

Beans and Barley Soup

2 (15 ounce) cans pinto beans with liquid	2 (425 g)
3 (14 ounce) cans chicken broth	3 (396 g)
½ cup quick-cooking barley	120 ml
1 (15 ounce) can Italian stewed tomatoes	425 g

- In 6-quart (6 L) slow cooker, combine beans, broth, barley, stewed tomatoes and ½ teaspoon (2 ml) pepper and stir well.
- Cover and cook on LOW for 4 to 5 hours.

■

Peachy Fruit Salad

2 (20 ounce) cans peach pie filling	2 (567 g)
1 (20 ounce) can pineapple chunks, drained	567 g
1 (11 ounce) can mandarin oranges, drained	312 g
1 (8 ounce) jar maraschino cherries, drained	227 g
1 cup miniature marshmallows	240 ml

- Combine all ingredients in large bowl, fold together gently and refrigerate.
- Serve in pretty crystal bowl. (Bananas may be added just before serving if you like.)

■ ■ ■

Potatoes and Salad

Cheesy Potato Soup

6 medium potatoes, peeled, cubed	
1 onion, very finely chopped	
2 (14 ounce) cans chicken broth	2 (396 g)
1 (8 ounce) package shredded American cheese	227 g
1 cup half-and-half cream	240 ml

- In slow cooker, combine potatoes, onion, chicken broth and ½ teaspoon (2 ml) pepper.
- Cover and cook on LOW for 8 to 10 hours. With potato masher, mash potatoes in slow cooker.
- About 1 hour before serving, stir in cheese and cream and cook 1 more hour.

TIP: *Use white pepper if you do not like black pepper specks in your soup.*

■

Broccoli-Green Bean Salad

1 large bunch broccoli, cut into florets	
2 (15 ounce) cans cut green beans, drained	2 (425 g)
1 bunch fresh green onions with tops, chopped	
2 (6 ounce) jars marinated artichoke hearts, chopped, drained	2 (168 g)
1½ cups ranch-style dressing (with mayonnaise)	360 ml

- Combine broccoli, green beans, onions and artichokes and mix well.
- Add dressing and toss and chill 24 hours before serving.

Potato Soup Supper

Garlic-Potato Soup

4 cups milk	1 L
1 (7 ounce) package roasted garlic instant mashed potatoes	198 g
1 (10 ounce) can cream of celery soup	280 g
1 (8 ounce) package shredded sharp cheddar cheese, divided	227 g
1 (4 ounce) can chopped pimentos	114 g

- Combine milk and 3 cups (710 ml) water in soup pot and bring to a boil. Remove from heat, add instant potato mix and stir with wire whisk until it mixes well. Stir in celery soup and mix well.

- Add half cheese, pimentos and ½ teaspoon (2 ml) pepper and stir until cheese melts. Ladle into individual bowls and sprinkle remaining cheese on top of each serving.

■

Spring Pear Salad Supper

1 (10 ounce) package spring salad mix	280 g
1 pound turkey, cut into thin strips	.5 kg
2 pears, cored, sliced	
1 cup Craisins® (dried cranberries)	
1 (8 ounce) bottle wild berry vinaigrette	227 g
2 tablespoons olive oil	30 ml
⅔ cup honey-roasted slivered almonds	160 ml

- In salad bowl, combine salad mix, turkey strips, pear and cranberries and chill.

- When ready to serve, spoon vinaigrette and olive oil over salad and toss. Sprinkle almonds over top of salad.

■ ■ ■

At-Home Time

At-Home Broccoli Soup

½ cup (½ stick) butter	120 ml
2 onions, finely chopped	
3 tablespoons flour	45 ml
3 (14 ounce) cans chicken broth	3 (396 g)
1 (16 ounce) package frozen chopped broccoli	.5 kg
1 cup shredded carrots	240 ml
1 (5 ounce) can evaporated milk	143 g

• Melt butter in soup pot and saute onions 5 to 6 minutes or until golden brown. Add flour and stir constantly until light brown. Stir in broth and bring to a boil; reduce heat, simmer for 10 minutes and stir constantly.

• Add broccoli and carrots and cook on medium heat for 10 minutes. Stir in evaporated milk and salt and pepper to taste. Heat just until soup is thoroughly hot.

■

Chicken Salad With Fruit

1 (12 ounce) package spring salad mix	340 g
1 (6 ounce) package frozen, ready-to-serve chicken strips, thawed	168 g
½ cup fresh raspberries	120 ml
½ cup fresh strawberries	120 ml
1 fresh peach, peeled, sliced	
1 (8 ounce) bottle raspberry salad dressing	227 g

• In salad bowl, combine salad mix, chicken strips, berries and peach slices. Toss with just enough salad dressing to coat salad. Serve immediately.

City-Slicker Soup Night

Pinto Bean-Vegetable Soup

4 (15 ounce) cans seasoned pinto beans with juice	4 (425 g)
1 (10 ounce) package frozen Seasoning Blend chopped onions and peppers	280 g
2 cups chopped celery	480 ml
2 (14 ounce) cans chicken broth	2 (396 g)
1 teaspoon Cajun seasoning	5 ml
⅛ teaspoon cayenne pepper	.5 ml

- Place all ingredients plus 1 cup (240 ml) water in 5-quart (5 L) slow cooker and stir well. Cover and cook on LOW 5 to 6 hours.

■

City-Slicker Salad

2 (10 ounce) packages fresh spinach	2 (280 g)
1 quart fresh strawberries, halved	1 L
½ cup slivered almonds, toasted	120 ml
Poppy seed dressing	

- Tear spinach into smaller pieces and add strawberries and almonds. Refrigerate until ready to serve. Toss with poppy seed dressing.

TIP: *Toasting brings out the flavor of almonds. Bake at 250°(121° C) for 10 minutes.*

Pepe's Special

Taco-Chili Soup

2 pounds very lean stew meat	1 kg
2 (15 ounce) cans Mexican stewed tomatoes	2 (425 g)
1 (1 ounce) package taco seasoning mix	28 g
2 (15 ounce) cans pinto beans with juice	2 (425 g)
1 (15 ounce) can whole kernel corn with juice	425 g

- Cut large pieces of stew meat in half and brown in large skillet. In 4 or 5-quart (4 L) slow cooker, combine stew meat, tomatoes, taco seasoning mix, beans, corn and ¾ cup (180 ml) water.
- Cover and cook on LOW for 5 to 7 hours. (If you are not into "spicy", use original recipe stewed tomatoes instead of Mexican.)

Creamy Orange Salad

1 (6 ounce) package orange gelatin	168 g
1 (8 ounce) package cream cheese, softened	227 g
1 (14 ounce) can sweetened condensed milk	396 g
1 (8 ounce) carton whipped topping	227 g
2 (11 ounce) cans mandarin orange slices, drained	2 (312 g)

- In bowl, dissolve gelatin in 1¼ (300 ml) cups boiling water. In mixing bowl, beat cream cheese until fluffy, gradually blend in hot gelatin and beat on low speed until smooth.
- Stir in condensed milk and refrigerate until mixture begins to thicken. Fold in whipped topping and orange slices. Spoon into 9 x 13-inch (23 x 33 cm) glass dish and refrigerate 4 hours before serving.

Speedy Gonzales' Favorite

Speedy Taco Soup

1 (12 ounce) can chicken with juice	340 g
1 (14 ounce) can chicken broth	396 g
1 (16 ounce) jar mild thick-and-chunky salsa	.5 kg
1 (15 ounce) can ranch-style beans	425 g

- Combine chicken, broth, salsa and beans in large saucepan. Bring to boil, reduce heat and simmer for 15 minutes.

TIP: A (15 ounce/425 g) can whole kernel corn may also be added.

■

Bread Sticks

1½ cups shredded Monterey Jack cheese	360 ml
¼ cup poppy seeds	60 ml
2 tablespoons dry onion soup mix	30 ml
2 (11 ounce) cans breadstick dough	2 (312 g)

- Spread cheese evenly in 9 x 13-inch (23 x 33 cm) baking dish. Sprinkle poppy seeds and soup mix evenly over cheese.
- Separate breadstick dough into sticks. Stretch strips slightly until each strip is about 12 inches (32 cm) long.
- Roll strips one at a time in cheese mixture and coat all sides.
- Cut into 3 or 4-inch (8 cm) strips. Place on cookie sheet and bake at 375° (190° C) for 12 minutes.

Beefy Soup Night

Beef-Noodle Soup

1 pound lean ground beef	.5 kg
1 (46 ounce) can cocktail vegetable juice	1.3 kg
1 (1 ounce) package onion soup mix	28 g
1 (3 ounce) package beef-flavored ramen noodles	84 g
1 (16 ounce) package frozen mixed vegetables	.5 kg

- In large saucepan, cook beef over medium heat until no longer pink and drain. Stir in vegetable juice, soup mix, noodle seasoning and mixed vegetables and bring to boil.
- Reduce heat and simmer, uncovered, for 6 minutes or until vegetables are tender. Return to boil and stir in noodles.
- Cook for 3 minutes or until noodles are tender and serve hot.

■

Corn Sticks

2 cups biscuit mix	480 ml
2 tablespoons minced green onions	30 ml
1 (8 ounce) can cream-style corn	227 g
Melted butter	

- Combine biscuit mix, green onions and cream-style corn.
- Place dough on floured surface and cut into 3 x 1-inch (8 x 2.5 cm) strips. Roll in melted butter.
- Bake at 400° (204° C) for 15 to 16 minutes.

Report For Duty

EDITORS CHOICE

Navy Bean Soup

3 (16 ounce) cans navy beans with juice	3 (.5 kg)
1 (14 ounce) can chicken broth	396 g
1 cup chopped ham	240 ml
1 large onion, chopped	
½ teaspoon garlic powder	2 ml

- In large saucepan, combine all ingredients with 1 cup (240 ml) water and bring to a boil.
- Simmer until onion is tender-crisp and serve hot with cheese muffins or cornbread.

■

Cheese Muffins

3¾ cups buttermilk-biscuit mix	890 ml
1¼ cups grated cheddar cheese	300 ml
1 egg, beaten	
1¼ cups milk	300 ml
Dash chili powder	

- In large bowl, combine all ingredients and beat vigorously by hand.
- Pour into greased muffin tins one-half to three-fourths full.
- Bake at 325° (162° C) for 35 minutes.

Easy Can-Opener Supper

Chili-Soup Warmer

1 (10 ounce) can tomato-bisque soup	280 g
1 (10 ounce) can chili	280 g
1 (10 ounce) can fiesta chili-beef soup	280 g
1 (15 ounce) can chicken broth	425 g

- In saucepan, combine all soups and broth. Add amount of water to produce desired thickness of soup.
- Heat and serve hot with crackers.

■

Bean Dip Express

1 (10 ounce) can black bean soup	280 g
1 (8 ounce) can tomato sauce	227 g
1 (8 ounce) carton sour cream	227 g
1 teaspoon chili powder	5 ml

- Mix soup and tomato sauce in saucepan over medium heat. Add sour cream and chili powder and mix well. Serve with chips and tortillas.

Hearty Heart-Warmers

Zesty Black Bean Soup

2 onions, finely chopped	
1 tablespoon chili powder	15 ml
2 teaspoons cumin	10 ml
3 (15 ounce) cans black beans with liquid	3 (425 g)
2 (14 ounce) cans beef broth	2 (396 g)

- Saute onions in soup pot with a little oil for 5 minutes and stir in chili powder and cumin.
- Puree 1 can beans and add to onion mixture. Add remaining beans and beef broth. Bring to a boil, reduce heat and simmer for 10 minutes. Before serving, garnish with shredded cheese or salsa.

■

Roasted Beef Salad Supper

¾ pound slice roast beef	340 g
1½ cups deli potato salad	360 ml
1 cup roasted sweet red bell peppers, cut in strips	240 ml
1 seedless cucumber, sliced	
1 small red onion, sliced into rings	

- Arrange roast beef slices and potato salad on platter and top with bell peppers, cucumber slices, onion rings and salt and pepper to taste. Cover and refrigerate overnight.

Dressing:

⅓ cup oil	80 ml
⅓ cup honey	80 ml
3 tablespoons red wine vinegar	45 ml
2 teaspoons minced parsley	10 ml
¼ teaspoon dill weed	1 ml

- Combine all dressing ingredients, mix well and pour over salad just before serving.

■ ■ ■

Soup and Salad Goodnight

Creamy Broccoli Soup

4 slices bacon	
1 small onion, finely chopped	
3 large potatoes, shredded	
1 (10 ounce) package frozen chopped broccoli	280 g
¼ cup (½ stick) butter	60 ml
3 tablespoons flour	45 ml
1 pint half-and-half cream	.5 ml

• Fry bacon in deep skillet, remove slices and drain on paper towels. When bacon cooks, crumble and set aside. With bacon drippings in skillet, add onion, potatoes, 2 cups (480 ml) water and 1 teaspoon (5 ml) salt. Cover and cook about 10 minutes. Add broccoli and cook additional 5 minutes.

• In separate large saucepan, melt butter, add flour and stir until bubbly. Gradually add cream and stir constantly until mixture thickens. Stir in potato-broccoli mixture and heat just until thoroughly hot. Sprinkle crumbled bacon on top of each serving.

■

Brown Rice Chicken Salad

1 (8.8 ounce) package whole-grain brown ready rice	255 g
1 (12 ounce) can premium chunk chicken breasts, drained	340 g
⅔ cup sun-dried tomatoes, chopped	160 ml
2 ripe avocados, peeled, diced	
¾ cup dijon-style mustard vinaigrette dressing	180 ml

• Prepare rice according to package directions. Combine rice, chicken, tomatoes, avocados and salt and pepper to taste. Spoon dressing over salad and gently toss to mix well. Chill at least 2 hours before serving.

■ ■ ■

Homemade Tomato Soup

3 (15 ounce) cans whole tomatoes with liquid	3 (425 g)
1 (14 ounce) can chicken broth	396 g
1 tablespoon sugar	15 ml
1 tablespoon minced garlic	15 ml
1 tablespoon balsamic vinegar	15 ml
¾ cup whipping cream	180 ml

- With blender, puree tomatoes (in batches) and pour into large saucepan. Add broth, sugar, garlic, vinegar and salt to taste and bring to a boil. Reduce heat, stir in cream and stir constantly for 2 to 3 minutes or until soup is thoroughly hot.

TIP: *If you have ready-cooked, crumbled bacon, sprinkle 1 tablespoon (15 ml) over each serving.*

■

Spinach and Turkey Salad Supper

2 (8 ounce) packages baby spinach, stems removed	2 (227 g)
½ cup walnuts halves	120 ml
½ cup Craisins® (dried cranberries)	120 ml
2 red delicious apples with peel, sliced	
1 pound smoked turkey, julienned	.5 kg
½ (15 ounce) bottle refrigerated honey-mustard dressing	½ (425 g)

- In large salad bowl, combine spinach, walnuts, craisins, apples and turkey. Toss salad with half honey-mustard dressing and add more if needed.

Supper In A Snap

Quick Spicy Tomato Soup

2 (10 ounce) cans tomato soup	2 (280 g)
1 (15 ounce) can Mexican-stewed tomatoes	425 g
Sour cream	
½ pound bacon, fried, drained, crumbled	227 g

- Combine soup and stewed tomatoes in saucepan and heat. To serve, spoon dollop of sour cream on top of soup and sprinkle crumbled bacon over sour cream.

■

Special Macaroni Salad

1 (16 ounce) carton prepared macaroni salad	.5 kg
1 (8 ounce) can whole kernel corn, drained	227 g
2 small zucchini, diced	
⅔ cup chunky salsa	160 ml

- In salad bowl with lid, combine macaroni salad, corn, zucchini and salsa and mix well. Cover and chill until ready to serve.

■

Salsa-Bean Dip

1 (15 ounce) can seasoned black beans, partially mashed	425 g
1 cup hot-and-chunky salsa	240 ml
3 fresh green onions with tops, chopped	
1 tablespoon olive oil	15 ml

- Place beans in shallow bowl and with fork mash about half. Stir in remaining ingredients. Chill several hours before serving with chips.

■ ■ ■

Soup and Salad

Swiss-Vegetable Soup

1 (1 ounce) package dry vegetable soup mix	28 g
1 cup half-and-half cream	240 ml
1½ cups shredded Swiss cheese	360 ml

- Combine soup mix and 3 cups (710 ml) water in saucepan and boil.
- Lower heat and simmer about 10 minutes. Add half-and-half cream and cheese and serve hot.

■

Caesar's Chicken Salad

4 boneless, skinless chicken breast halves, grilled	
1 (10 ounce) package romaine salad greens	280 g
½ cup shredded parmesan cheese	120 ml
1 cup seasoned croutons	240 ml

- Cut chicken breasts into strips. Combine chicken, salad greens, cheese and croutons in large bowl.
- When ready to serve, toss with ¾ cup (180 ml) Caesar or Italian dressing.

■ ■ ■

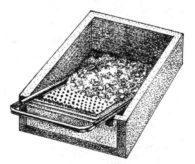

Don't Blow It

Easy Chili

2 pounds lean ground beef	1 kg
1 onion, chopped	
4 (16 ounce) cans chili-hot beans with liquid	4 (.5 kg)
1 (1.5 ounce) package chili seasoning mix	45 g
1 (46 ounce) can tomato juice	1.3 kg

- Cook beef and onion in Dutch oven, stir until meat crumbles and drain.
- Stir in remaining ingredients. Bring mixture to boil, reduce heat and simmer, stirring occasionally, for 2 hours.

■

Chile Bread

1 loaf unsliced Italian bread	
½ cup (1 stick) butter, melted	120 ml
1 (4 ounce) can diced green chilies, drained	114 g
¾ cup grated Monterey Jack cheese	180 ml

- Slice bread almost through. Combine melted butter, chilies and cheese. Spread between bread slices.
- Cover loaf with foil. Bake at 350° (176° C) for 15 minutes.

Home Sweet Home

Comfort Stew

1½ pounds select stew meat	.7 kg
2 (10 ounce) cans French onion soup	2 (280 g)
1 (10 ounce) can cream of onion soup	280 g
1 (10 ounce) can cream of celery soup	280 g
1 (16 ounce) package frozen stew vegetables, thawed	.5 kg

- Place stew meat in bottom of sprayed slow cooker. Add soups in order given and spread evenly over meat. DO NOT STIR.
- Turn slow cooker to HIGH and cook just long enough for ingredients to get hot.
- Change heat setting to LOW, cover and cook for 7 to 8 hours.

■

Sunflower Salad

2 apples, cored, chopped	
1 cup seedless green grapes, halved	240 ml
½ cup chopped celery	120 ml
¾ cup chopped pecans	180 ml
⅓ cup mayonnaise	80 ml

- Combine all ingredients and chill.

■ ■ ■

Cornbread Night

Easy Pork Stew

This is great with cornbread!

1 (1 pound) pork tenderloin, cubed	.5 kg
2 (12 ounce) jars pork gravy	2 (340 g)
¼ cup chili sauce	60 ml
1 (16 ounce) package frozen stew vegetables, thawed	.5 kg

- Cook pork pieces in greased soup pot on medium-high heat for 10 minutes, stirring frequently.
- Stir in gravy, chili sauce and stew vegetables and bring to boil. Reduce heat and simmer for 12 minutes or until vegetables are tender.

■

Cheddar Cornbread

2 (8 ounce) packages cornbread-muffin mix	2 (227 g)
2 eggs, beaten	
1 cup plain yogurt	240 ml
1 (14 ounce) can cream-style corn	396 g
½ cup shredded cheddar cheese	120 ml

- In bowl, combine cornbread mix, eggs and yogurt and blend well. Stir in corn and cheese.
- Pour into greased 9 x 13-inch (23 x 33 cm) baking dish. Bake at 400° (204° C) for 18 to 20 minutes or until light brown.

Santa Fe Hot Shot

Santa Fe Stew

1½ pounds lean ground beef	.7 kg
1 (14 ounce) can beef broth	396 g
1 (15 ounce) can whole kernel corn with juice	425 g
2 (15 ounce) cans pinto beans with juice	2 (425 g)
2 (15 ounce) cans Mexican stewed tomatoes	2 (425 g)
1 tablespoon beef seasoning	15 ml
1 (16 ounce) carton cubed processed cheese	.5 kg

- In skillet, brown beef until no longer pink. Place in 5 to 6-quart (5 L) slow cooker and add broth, corn, beans, tomatoes and beef seasoning.
- Cook on LOW for 5 to 6 hours. When ready to serve, fold in cheese chunks and stir until cheese melts.

TIP: *Cornbread is a must to serve with this stew. There are several cornbread receipes on pages 24, 26 & 53.*

■

Sesame-Romaine Salad

1 large head romaine lettuce	
2 tablespoons sesame seeds, toasted	30 ml
6 strips bacon, fried, crumbled	
½ cup grated Swiss cheese	120 ml

- Wash and dry lettuce. Tear into bite-size pieces. When ready to serve, sprinkle sesame seeds, bacon and cheese over lettuce and toss with creamy Italian salad dressing.

Reuben's Special

EDITORS CHOICE

Reuben Casserole Supper

1 (20 ounce) bag frozen hash brown potatoes, thawed	567 g
1½ pounds deli corned beef slices, ¼-inch thick	360 ml/.6 cm
1 (8 ounce) bottle Russian salad dressing	227 g
1 (15 ounce) can sauerkraut, drained	425 g
8 slices Swiss cheese	

- Preheat oven to 400° (204° C). Place hash brown potatoes in sprayed 9 x 13-inch (23 x 33 cm) backing dish and season with salt and pepper. Bake uncovered for 30 minutes.
- Place corned beef slices overlapping on top of potatoes. Spoon half bottle of dressing over top of beef and arrange sauerkraut on top.
- Cover with slices of cheese, reduce heat to 350° (176° C) and bake another 15 minutes.

■

Colorful Salad Toss

2 (8 ounce) packages baby spinach, stems removed	2 (227 g)
1 small head cauliflower, cut into small florets	
1 red bell pepper, seeded, chopped	
¾ cup walnut halves	180 ml
½ cup roasted sunflower seeds	120 ml
1 (8 ounce) bottle wild berry vinaigrette salad dressing	227 g

- In large salad bowl, combine spinach, cauliflower, bell pepper strips, walnuts, sunflower seeds and generous amount of salt. Chill.
- Pour about half salad dressing over salad and toss; add more dressing if needed.

■ ■ ■

Sunday Night Lights

Cabbage and Bean Salad

1 (16 ounce) package coleslaw mix	.5 kg
2 (15 ounce) cans garbanzo beans, rinsed, drained	2 (425 g)
1 (15 ounce) can kidney beans, rinsed, drained	425 g
1 (8 ounce) bottle zesty Italian salad dressing	227 g

- In large salad bowl with lid, combine coleslaw mix and all 3 cans beans. Pour salad dressing over mixture and toss.
- Refrigerate several hours before serving. Serve with slotted spoon.

■

Sunday-Night-Lights

2 (15 ounce) cans chili without beans	2 (425 g)
2 (15 ounce) cans pinto beans with liquid	2 (425 g)
2 (15 ounce) cans beef tamales, shucks removed	2 (425 g)
1 (8 ounce) package shredded Mexican 4-cheese blend, divided	227 g

- Preheat oven to 350° (176° C). In greased 9 x 13-inch (23 x 33 cm) baking pan, spoon both cans chili on bottom of pan and spread out with back of large spoon. Spread beans with liquid over top. Spread all tamales over beans. Sprinkle about ½ cup (120 ml) cheese over top, cover and bake 30 minutes.
- Remove from oven, sprinkle remaining cheese over top of casserole and return to oven for just 5 minutes. Serve with lots of tortilla chips.

TIP: *You might want to serve some hot thick-and-chunky salsa along with this dish.*

Pasta Time

Terrific Tortellini Salad

2 (14 ounce) packages frozen cheese tortellini   2 (680 g)
1 green and 1 red bell pepper, diced
1 cucumber, chopped
1 (14 ounce) can artichoke hearts, rinsed, drained   396 g
1 (8 ounce) bottle creamy Caesar salad dressing   227 g

- Prepare tortellini according to package directions and drain. Rinse with cold water, drain and chill.
- Combine tortellini, bell peppers, cucumber, artichoke hearts and dressing in large bowl. Cover and refrigerate at least 2 hours before serving.

■

Garlic Toast

1 loaf French bread	
1 tablespoon garlic powder	15 ml
2 tablespoons dried parsley flakes	30 ml
½ cup (1 stick) butter, melted	120 ml
1 cup grated parmesan cheese	240 ml

- Slice bread into 1-inch (2.5 cm) slices diagonally. In small bowl combine rest of ingredients except cheese and mix well.
- Use brush to spread mixture on bread slices and sprinkle with parmesan cheese. Place on cookie sheet and bake at 225° (107° C) for about 1 hour.

Pasta Please

Pasta Plus Salad

1 (16 ounce) package bow-tie pasta	.5 kg
1 (10 ounce) package frozen green peas, thawed	280 g
1 red bell pepper, seeded, cut in strips	
1 (8 ounce) package cubed Swiss cheese	227 g
1 small yellow summer squash, sliced	
1 (8 ounce) bottle ranch dressing	227 g

- Cook pasta according to package directions and add peas last 2 minutes of cooking time. Drain pasta and peas, rinse in cold water and drain again. Transfer to large salad bowl and add bell pepper, cheese and squash.
- Spoon dressing over salad with a little salt and pepper to taste. Toss salad with dressing and chill.

■

Beef Patties With Mushroom Gravy

1 pound lean ground beef	.5 kg
¼ cup chili sauce	60 ml
1 egg	
¾ cup crushed cornflakes	180 ml
2 (10 ounce) can cream of mushroom soup	2 (280 g)

- In bowl, combine ground beef, chili sauce, egg, crushed cornflakes and salt and pepper to taste and mix well. Shape into 4 patties about ¾-inch (1.8 cm) thick.
- Place patties in skillet with tiny bit of oil and brown each patty on high heat on both sides. Reduce heat to medium; stir in both cans soup with ½ cup (120 ml) water and mix well. Spoon gravy over patties and simmer for about 25 minutes.

Bowl Game

Pasta Salad Bowl

1 (16 ounce) package bow-tie pasta	.5 kg
1 (16 ounce) package frozen green peas, thawed	.5 kg
½ cup sliced fresh green onions	120 ml
1 seed less cucumber, thinly sliced	
2 cups deli ham, cut in strips	480 ml

• Cook pasta according to package directions and drain. Cool under cold running water and drain again. Transfer to serving bowl and add peas, onions, cucumber and ham.

Dressing:

⅔ cup mayonnaise	160 ml
¼ cup cider vinegar	60 ml
1 teaspoon sugar	5ml
2 teaspoons dried dill	10 ml

• In small bowl, combine dressing ingredients and spoon over salad. Toss to coat well and chill.

■

Spinach Soup

2 (10 ounce) packages frozen chopped spinach, cooked	2 (280 g)
2 (10 ounce) cans cream of mushroom soup	2 (280 g)
1 cup half-and-half cream	240 ml
1 (14 ounce) can chicken broth	396 g

• Puree spinach, soup and cream in blender until smooth. Combine spinach mixture and broth in saucepan and heat on medium heat until it blends well. Reduce heat to low and simmer for 20 minutes. Serve hot or cold.

■ ■ ■

Ready Or Not

Supper-Ready Beef and Bean Salad

¾ pound deli roast beef, cut in strips   340 g
2 (15 ounce) cans kidney beans, rinsed, drained   2 (425 g)
1 cup chopped onion   240 ml
1 cup chopped celery   240 ml
3 eggs, hard-boiled, chopped

- In salad bowl, combine all salad ingredients.

Dressing:

⅓ cup mayonnaise   80 ml
⅓ cup chipotle chili gourmayo   80 ml
¼ cup ketchup   60 ml
¼ cup sweet pickle relish   60 ml
2 tablespoons olive oil   30 ml

- In small bowl, combine dressing ingredients and mix well. Spoon over beef-bean mixture and toss. Chill several hours before serving. Shred lettuce on serving plate and spoon beef-bean salad over lettuce to serve.

■

Quick-Corn-On-The-Cob

1 fresh ear corn-on-the -cob
Butter

- Microwave 1 ear of corn in its husk for 2 minutes on HIGH. (Silky threads come off more easily after corn cooks.) Turn once and halfway through cooking.
- Remove husk and silks, wrap ear in wax paper, cook 2 minutes on HIGH. Turn once after 1 minute. For multiple ears, double or triple time for 2 or 3 ears.

TIP: *The easiest way to cook corn-on-the-cob is to boil it, but the quickest way is to microwave it.*

■ ■ ■

A Great Way To Eat Lettuce

Taco Salad

1½ pounds lean ground beef	.7 kg
1 onion, chopped	
2 teaspoons chili powder	10 ml
½ teaspoon ground cumin	2 ml
¾ head lettuce, chopped	
3 tomatoes, chopped	
1 (16 ounce) package shredded Mexican 4-cheese blend, divided	.5 kg
1 (10 ounce) package original corn chips	280 g

- In skillet, brown beef and onion; add chili powder and cumin. When ready to serve, place lettuce, tomatoes and about 8 ounces (227 g) cheese in large salad bowl.
- Spoon beef-onion mixture over salad, add remaining cheese and chips and toss.

■

Easy Cheesy Bean Dip

1 (15 ounce) can refried beans	425 g
1 teaspoon minced garlic	5 ml
1 cup milk	240 ml
1 (16 ounce) package Mexican processed cheese	.5 kg

- Combine beans, garlic and milk and stir on low heat until smooth. Cut cheese in chunks and add to bean mixture. On low heat, stir until cheese melts. Serve warm with chips.

TIP: *Something else that's good is to spread bean dip on flour tortillas, add chopped tomatoes, chopped jalapenos and grated cheese, roll up and pig out.*

Easy, Short-Cut Classics

Chicken Salad

3 cups cooked, chopped, boneless, skinless chicken breast halves,	710 ml
1½ cups chopped celery	360 ml
½ cup sweet pickle relish	120 ml
2 eggs, hard-boiled, chopped	
¾ cup mayonnaise	180 ml

- Combine all ingredients and several sprinkles salt and pepper. Serve over lettuce leaf or as sandwiches.

■

Tomato-French Onion Soup

1 (10 ounce) can tomato-bisque soup	280 g
2 (10 ounce) cans French-onion soup	2 (280 g)
Grated parmesan cheese	
Croutons	

- In saucepan, combine soups and 2 soup cans water. Heat thoroughly.
- Serve in bowls topped with croutons and a sprinkle of cheese.

■ ■ ■

Dessert's The Best

Light Chicken Salad Supper

1 rotisserie-cooked chicken	
1 cup halved red and green grapes	240 ml
2 cups chopped celery	480 ml
⅔ cup walnut halves	160 ml
⅔ cup sliced onion	160 ml

- Skin chicken, cut chicken breast in thin strips and place in bowl with lid. Add remaining ingredients.

Dressing:

½ cup mayonnaise	120 ml
1 tablespoon orange juice	15 ml
2 tablespoons red wine vinegar	30 ml
1 teaspoon chili powder	5 ml
1 teaspoon paprika	5 ml

- Combine all dressing ingredients, add salt and pepper to taste and mix well. Spoon over salad mixture and toss. Chill.

■

Cinnamon-Apple Cobbler

2 (20 ounce) cans apple pie filling	2 (567 g)
½ cup packed brown sugar	120 ml
1½ teaspoons cinnamon	7 ml
1 (18 ounce) box yellow cake mix	510 g
½ cup (1 stick) butter, melted	120 ml

- Preheat oven to 350° (176° C). Spread apple pie filling in bottom of sprayed 9 x 13-inch (23 x 33 cm) baking dish.
- Sprinkle with brown sugar and cinnamon and top with dry cake mix. Drizzle melted butter over top. Bake for 50 minutes or until light brown and bubbly.

■ ■ ■

Get Your Vegetables

Broccoli-Chicken Salad

3 - 4 boneless, skinless chicken breast halves, cooked, cubed	
2 cups fresh broccoli florets	480 ml
1 red bell pepper, seeded, chopped	
1 cup chopped celery	240 ml

- Combine chicken, broccoli, bell pepper and celery. Toss with honey-mustard dressing and refrigerate.

■

Easy Potato Soup

1 (16 ounce) package frozen hash brown potatoes	.5 kg
1 cup chopped onion	240 ml
1 (14 ounce) can chicken broth	396 g
1 (10 ounce) can cream of celery	280 g
1 (10 ounce) can cream of chicken soup	280 g
2 cups milk	480 ml

- Combine potatoes, onion and 2 cups (480 ml) water in large saucepan and bring to boil.
- Cover, reduce heat and simmer 30 minutes. Stir in broth, soups and milk and heat thoroughly.

TIP: *If you like, garnish with shredded cheddar cheese or diced, cooked ham.*

Chow-Down Chowder

Chicken-Artichoke Salad

4 cups cooked, chopped chicken breasts	1 L
1 (14 ounce) can artichoke hearts, drained chopped	396 g
½ cup chopped walnuts	120 ml
1 cup chopped, seeded red bell pepper	240 ml
⅔ cup mayonnaise	160 ml

- In bowl, combine all ingredients with salt and pepper to taste. Cover and chill until ready to serve.

TIP: *This can be a hot salad if you place a lot of salad on slices of toasted Texas toast. Sprinkle it with shredded cheddar cheese and bake at 400° (204° C) for 10 minutes. A hot salad for a cold night!*

■

Quick Corn Chowder

2 baking potatoes, peeled, diced	
½ cup finely chopped onion	120 ml
1 (15 ounce) can cream-style corn	425 g
1 (8 ounce) can whole kernel corn	227 g
1 (10 ounce) can cream of celery soup	280 g
1 cup milk	240 ml
1 (8 ounce) package cubed processed cheese	

- In large saucepan, cook potatoes and onion in 1½ cups (360 ml) water about 15 minutes or until potatoes are tender; do not drain. Stir in cream-style corn, whole kernel corn, celery soup, milk and salt and pepper to taste. Heat, stir constantly until mixture is thoroughly hot and stir in cheese.

TIP: *Herbed croutons make a nice garnish if you have them in the pantry.*

Around The World

Luscious Papaya-Chicken Salad

1 (10 ounce) package torn romaine lettuce leaves	280 g
2 ripe papayas, peeled, seeded, cubed	
1 large red bell pepper, seeded, chopped	
2 cups cooked, cubed chicken breasts	480 ml
½ cup chopped pecans, toasted	120 ml

Dressing:

½ cup lime juice	120 ml
⅓ cup honey	80 ml
2 teaspoons minced garlic	10 ml
3 tablespoons extra-virgin oil	45 ml

- In large salad bowl, combine lettuce, papayas and bell pepper. In small bowl, whisk lime juice, honey and garlic. Slowly add olive oil and whisk dressing until it blends well. Pour dressing over salad, add cubed chicken and pecans; toss.

■

Mexican-Style Minestrone Soup

1 (16 ounce) package frozen garlic-seasoned pasta and vegetables	.5 kg
1 (16 ounce) jar thick-and-chunky salsa	.5 kg
1 (15 ounce) can pinto beans with liquid	425 g
1 teaspoon chili powder	5 ml
1 teaspoon cumin	5 ml
1 (8 ounce) package shredded Mexican-style 4-cheese blend	227 g

- In large saucepan, combine all ingredients except cheese with 1 cup (240 ml) water. Bring to a boil, reduce heat and simmer for 8 minutes. Stir often and top each serving with cheese.

■ ■ ■

Aloha Night

Hawaiian Chicken Salad

3 cups cooked, diced chicken breasts	710 ml
1 (20 ounce) can pineapple tidbits, well drained	567 g
1 cup halved red grapes	240 ml
3 ribs celery, sliced	
1 large ripe banana, sliced	

Dressing:

½ cup mayonnaise	120 ml
¾ cup poppy seed dressing	180 ml
½ cup salted peanuts	120 ml

- In bowl, combine chicken, pineapple, grapes and celery and toss. Cover and chill.
- Combine mayonnaise, poppy seed dressing and salt to taste. When ready to serve, add bananas and top with mayonnaise-poppy seed dressing and toss.
- Just before serving, sprinkle peanuts over top of salad.

■

Popovers

1 cup flour	240 ml
2 eegs	
1 cup milk	240 ml
1 tablespoon shortening, melted	15 ml

- Preheat oven to 425°(220° C). Combine all ingredients and mix until smooth. Fill 6 sprayed custard cups about half full. Bake for 40 minutes or until puffed and light brown.

Healthy Choices

Spinach and Chicken Salad

1 (10 ounce) package baby spinach	280 g
1 seedless cucumber, sliced	
1 red delicious apple, unpeeled, thinly sliced	
1 bunch green onions with tops, sliced	
3 cups coarsely shredded rotisserie chicken meat	710 ml

" In salad bowl, combine spinach, cucumber, apple, green onions and chicken; toss to mix well.

Dressing:

⅓ cup red wine vinegar	80 ml
3 tablespoons olive oil	45 ml
1 tablespoon dijon-style mustard	15 ml
1 teaspoon sugar	5 ml

" In saucepan combine all dressing ingredients and heat just until thoroughly hot. Pour over salad and toss so salad coats evenly. Serve immediately.

■

Easy Gazpacho

2 (28 ounce) cans diced tomatoes	2 (794 g)
1 seedless cumber with peel, cubed	
1 cup cubed red onion	240 ml
1 cup cubed celery	240 ml
2 serrano chile peppers, seeded, coarsely chopped	

" Working in batches, combine all ingredients plus salt and pepper to taste in food processor or blender and pulse until mixture is thick soup.

TIP: *For an added touch, garnish with several lemon slices.*

■ ■ ■

Salad Special

Herbed Chicken Salad

1 rotisserie-cooked chicken	
¼ cup chopped fresh chives	60 ml
2 tablespoons capers	30 ml
1 cup chopped celery	240 ml
1 cup chopped sweet pickles	240 ml

- Skin chicken and cut meat from bones. Slice chicken in thin strips and place in bowl. Add remaining ingredients and mix well.

Dressing:

1 tablespoon honey	15 ml
¼ cup extra-virgin olive oil	60 ml
3 tablespoons white wine vinegar	45 ml
1 teaspoon chopped fresh thyme	5 ml
1 teaspoon chopped fresh oregano	5 ml

- In bowl whisk all dressing ingredients plus salt and pepper to taste. Spoon over chicken salad and toss. Chill.

■

Creamy Broccoli-Rice Soup

1 (6 ounce) package chicken and wild rice mix	168 g
1 (10 ounce) package frozen chopped broccoli	280 g
2 (10 ounce) cans cream of chicken soup	2 (280 g)
1 (12 ounce) can chicken breast chunks	340 g

- In soup pot, combine rice mix, contents of seasoning packet and 5 cups (1.3 L) water. Bring to a boil, reduce heat and simmer for 15 minutes.
- Stir in broccoli, chicken soup and chicken, cover and simmer for another 5 minutes.

■ ■ ■

Chicken Salad Switch

Black Bean Chicken Salad

3 - 4 boneless, skinless chicken breasts, cooked, cubed
1 (15 ounce) can black beans, drained   425 g
1 bunch green onions, chopped
1 cup chopped celery   240 ml

- Blend all ingredients and toss with Cumin-Vinaigrette Dressing below.

Cumin-Vinaigrette Dressing:

¾ cup virgin olive oil   180 ml
¼ cup lemon juice   60 ml
2 teaspoons dijon-style mustard   10 ml
2 teaspoons ground cumin   10 ml

- Combine all ingredients. Toss with black beans and chicken salad and refrigerate.

■

Oven Fries

5 medium baking potatoes
⅓ cup oil   80 ml
Paprika

- Scrub potatoes, cut each in 6 lengthwise wedges and place in shallow baking dish.
- Combine oil, ¾ teaspoon (4 ml) salt and ¼ teaspoon (1 ml) pepper and brush potatoes with mixture. Sprinkle potatoes lightly with paprika.
- Bake at 375° (190° C) for about 50 minutes or until potatoes are tender and light brown. Baste twice with remaining oil mixture while baking.

■ ■ ■

Express Salad

Apple-Walnut Chicken Salad

3 - 4 boneless, skinless chicken breast halves, cooked, cubed	
2 tart green apples, peeled, chopped	
½ cup chopped pitted dates	120 ml
1 cup finely chopped celery	240 ml

- Mix all ingredients. Toss with dressing.

Dressing:

½ cup chopped walnuts	120 ml
⅓ cup sour cream	80 ml
⅓ cup mayonnaise	80 ml
1 tablespoon lemon juice	15 ml

- Toast walnuts at 300° (148° C) for 10 minutes. Mix sour cream, mayonnaise and lemon juice. Mix with walnuts. Pour over chicken salad and toss. Refrigerate.

■

Cheese Drops

2 cups baking mix	480 ml
⅔ cup milk	160 ml
⅔ cup grated sharp cheddar cheese	160 ml
¼ cup (½ stick) butter, melted	60 ml

- Mix baking mix, milk and cheese. Drop 1 heaping tablespoon (15 ml) dough for each biscuit onto greased baking sheet.
- Bake at 400° (204° C) for 10 minutes or until slightly brown. While warm, brush tops of biscuits with melted butter. Serve hot.

■ ■ ■

Derby Night

Derby Day Toss

**3 - 4 boneless, skinless chicken breast halves,
   cooked, cubed**
¼ pound bacon, cooked, crumbled   114 g
2 avocados, peeled, diced
2 tomatoes, diced, drained

- Combine all ingredients.
- When ready to serve, pour Italian dressing over salad and toss.
  Refrigerate.

■

Butter Rolls

2 cups biscuit mix   480 ml
1 (8 ounce) carton sour cream   227 g
½ cup (1 stick) butter, melted   120 ml

- Combine all ingredients and mix well. Spoon into greased muffin tins half full.
- Bake at 400° (204° C) for 12 to 14 minutes or until light brown.

Quick Chicken and Salad

Chicken Quesadillas

3 boneless, skinless chicken breast halves, cubed
1 (10 ounce) can cheddar cheese soup   **280 g**
⅔ cup chunky salsa   **160 ml**
10 flour tortillas

- Cook chicken in skillet until juices evaporate and stir often. Add soup and salsa and heat thoroughly.
- Spread about ⅓ cup (80 ml) soup mixture on half tortilla to within ½-inch (1.2 cm) of edge. Moisten edge with water, fold over and seal. Place tortillas on 2 baking sheets.
- Bake at 400° (204° C) for 5 to 6 minutes.

■

Broccoli-Pepperoni Salad

1 (1 pound) bunch broccoli   **.5 kg**
½ pound fresh mushrooms, sliced   **227 g**
6 ounces Swiss cheese, diced   **168 g**
1 (3 ounce) package sliced pepperoni, chopped   **84 g**

- Cut off broccoli florets and combine broccoli, mushrooms, cheese and pepperoni.
- Toss with Italian dressing. Refrigerate at least 8 hours before serving.

■ ■ ■

Almost Instant Supper

Noodle-Turkey Salad

1 (3 ounce) package oriental-flavor ramen noodle soup mix	84 g
1 (16 ounce) package finely shredded coleslaw mix	.5 kg
¾ pound smoked turkey, cut into strips	340 g
½ cup vinaigrette salad dressing	120 ml

- Coarsely crush noodles and place in bowl with lid. Add coleslaw mix and turkey strips.
- In small bowl, combine vinaigrette salad dressing and seasoning packet from noodle mix, pour over noodle-turkey mixture and toss to coat mixture well. Chill before serving.

■

French Cheese Loaf

1 (14 ounce) loaf unsliced French bread	396 g
½ cup (1 stick) butter, softened	120 ml
1 teaspoon prepared minced garlic	5 ml
1 (4 ounce) package crumbled blue cheese	114 g

- Preheat oven to 375° (190° C). Slice bread into 1-inch (2.5 cm) slices, but do not cut through bottom of loaf.
- In bowl, combine butter, garlic and blue cheese and spread evenly on both sides of each bread slice. Wrap loaf in foil and place on large baking pan. Bake 10 to 12 minutes or until bread is hot.

Great Turkey

Asian Turkey Salad

¾ pound turkey breasts, julienned	340 g
1 (9 ounce) package coleslaw mix	255 g
¼ cup chopped fresh cilantro	60 ml
1 sweet red bell pepper, seeded, julienned	
1 bunch fresh green onions, sliced	

- In salad bowl, combine all ingredients.

Dressing:

¼ cup olive oil	60 ml
2 tablespoons lime juice	30 ml
1 tablespoon sugar	15 ml
1 tablespoon peanut butter	15 ml
1 tablespoon soy sauce	15 ml

- In jar with lid, combine all dressing ingredients, seal jar and shake until dressing blends well. Spoon over salad and toss. Serve immediately.

■

Tomato-Bean Soup

2 tablespoon oil	30 ml
1 (16 ounce) package frozen chopped onion and peppers	.5 kg
2 ribs celery, sliced	
2 (15 ounce) cans pork and beans	2 (425 g)
1 (15 ounce) can stewed tomatoes	425 g
2 cups chopped ham	480 ml

- In soup pot, combine oil, chopped onion and peppers and celery, cook on medium heat for 5 minutes and stir often. Fold in pork and beans, tomatoes, ham and salt to taste. Cook for 10 to 15 minutes on low heat and stir once.

■ ■ ■

Soup Surprise

Pasta-Turkey Salad Supper

1 (12 ounce) package tri-color spiral pasta	340 g
1 (4 ounce) can sliced ripe olives, drained	114 g
2 cups fresh broccoli florets, chopped	480 ml
2 small yellow squash, sliced	
1 (3 pounce) package hickory-smoked cracked	
pepper turkey breast, sliced	1.3 kg
1 (8 ounce) bottle cheddar-parmesan ranch dressing	227 g

- Cook pasta according to package directions, drain and rinse in cold water. Place in large salad bowl and add olives, broccoli and squash.
- Pour dressing over salad mixture and toss. Place turkey on top of salad.

TIP: *You won't need all the turkey, but what's left will make great sandwiches!*

■

So Easy Peanut Soup

2 (10 ounce) cans cream of chicken soup	2 (280 g)
2 soups cans milk	
1¼ cups crunchy-style peanut butter	300 ml

- In saucepan, blend soup and milk on medium heat. Stir in peanut butter and heat until it blends. Serve hot.

■ ■ ■

Suddenly Salad

Sunny Ham Salad

3 cups chopped ham	710 ml
1 bunch fresh green onions with tops, chopped	
½ cup silvered almonds, toasted	120 ml
½ cup sunflower seeds	120 ml
2 cups chopped fresh broccoli florets	480 ml
¾ cup mayonnaise	180 ml

- Combine chopped ham, green onions, almonds, sunflower seeds and broccoli florets.
- Toss with mayonnaise. Refrigerate. Serve on lettuce leaves, or stuff in hollowed out tomato.

■

Terrific Taters

5 - 6 medium potatoes	
1 (8 ounce) carton sour cream	227 g
1 (1 ounce) package dry ranch-style dressing mix	28 g
1½ cups shredded cheddar cheese	360 ml
3 pieces bacon, fried, drained, crumbled	

- Peel, slice and boil potatoes until tender and drain. Place potatoes in 2-quart (2 L) baking dish.
- Combine sour cream, salad dressing mix and a little pepper. Toss until potatoes coat well. Sprinkle cheese on top. Bake at 350° (176° C) for about 20 minutes. Sprinkle bacon on top and serve hot.

Wacky World

Wacky Tuna Salad

2 (7 ounce) packages cooked light tuna in water	2 (198 g)
1 red apple with peel, cored, chopped	
1 (10 ounce) package frozen green peas, thawed, drained	280 g
1 sweet red bell pepper, chopped	
½ (8 ounce) bottle sweet honey Catalina salad dressing	½ (227 g)
½ cup mayonnaise	120 ml

- Combine tuna, apple, peas and bell peppers and toss. In bowl combine dressing and mayonnaise, spoon over salad; toss. Chill 2 hours and serve over bed of shredded lettuce.

■

Supper Frittata

2 cups cooked white rice	480 ml
1 (10 ounce) box frozen green peas, thawed	280 g
1 cup cooked, cubed ham	240 ml
8 large eggs, beaten	
1 cup shredded pepper Jack cheese, divided	240 ml
1 teaspoon dried thyme	5 ml

- In large ovenproof skillet with a little oil, heat rice, peas and ham 4 minutes or until mixture is thoroughly hot. In separate bowl, whisk eggs, three-fourths of cheese, thyme and salt to taste. Add to mixture in skillet and shake skillet gently to distribute evenly. On medium heat, cover and cook, without stirring, until mixture sets on bottom and sides. (Eggs will still be runny in center.)
- Sprinkle remaining cheese over top. Place skillet in oven and broil about 5 minutes or until frittata is firm in center.

■ ■ ■

Tortellini for Famillini

Tuna-Tortellini Salad

1 (7 ounce) package cut spaghetti	198 g
¼ cup (½ stick) butter	60 ml
1 (12 ounce) can tuna, drained	340 g
1 (4 ounce) can sliced ripe olives	114 g

- Cook spaghetti according to package directions, drain, add butter and stir until butter melts. Add tuna and olives.

Dressing:

¾ cup whipping cream	180 ml
1 teaspoon dried basil leaves	5 ml
2 tablespoons grated parmesan cheese	30 ml

- Combine dressing ingredients with 1 teaspoon (5 ml) salt. Pour over spaghetti-tuna mixture and toss.

■

Pina Colada Pie

2 pints vanilla ice cream, softened	1 kg
1 (15 ounce) can crushed pineapple, drained	425 g
½ cup flaked coconut	120 ml
2 tablespoons light rum	30 ml

- Place ice cream in large bowl, stir in pineapple, coconut and rum and mix well. Spoon into 9-inch (23 cm) graham cracker piecrust and freeze. Let pie stand at room temperature about 10 minutes before slicing.

TIP: *Soften ice cream in refrigerator for about 30 minutes.*

Summer Night's Breeze

Tuna-Stuffed Tomatoes

4 large tomatoes	
2 (6 ounce) cans white meat tuna, drained	2 (168 g)
2 cups chopped celery	480 ml
½ cup chopped cashews	120 ml
1 small zucchini with peel, finely chopped	
½ cup mayonnaise	120 ml

- Cut thin slice off top of each tomato, scoop out pulp and discard. Turn tomatoes, top down, on paper towels to drain.
- Combine tuna, celery, cashews, zucchini, mayonnaise and a little salt and pepper to taste and mix well. Spoon mixture into hollowed-out tomatoes. Refrigerate.

■

Cheese-Biscuit Bandits

1 (6 ounce) jar Old English cheese	168 g
1 cup (2 sticks) butter	240 ml
½ teaspoon cayenne pepper	2 ml
¼ teaspoon baking powder	1 ml
2⅓ cups flour	560 ml
1 cup very finely chopped pecans	240 ml

- With mixer, blend cheese and butter. Add 1 teaspoon (2 ml) salt, cayenne pepper, baking powder and flour and mix well. (Dough will be very stiff.) Stir in pecans.
- Make 4 logs about 8 inches (20 cm) long. Wrap in wax paper and chill in refrigerator until ready to bake. Cut slices [⅛-inch (.4 cm) thick and place on lightly greased baking sheet. Bake at 325° (162° C) for about 20 minutes.

Meatball Hoagies

1 small onion, diced
1 small green bell pepper, diced
1 (15 ounce) can sloppy Joe sauce   425 g
30 - 32 frozen cooked meatballs
4 hoagie buns

- Saute onion and pepper in 1 tablespoon (15 ml) oil. Add sauce and meatballs, cook 10 minutes or until thoroughly hot and stir often. Spoon evenly onto hoagie buns.

■

Tumbleweeds

1 (12 ounce) package butterscotch chips   340 g
¼ cup peanut butter   60 ml
1 (12 ounce) can peanuts   340 g
1 (4 ounce) can shoestring potatoes   114 g

- In saucepan on low heat, melt chips with peanut butter and mix well.
- Stir in peanuts and shoestring potatoes. Drop by tablespoonfuls on wax paper. Store in airtight container.

■ ■ ■

Cheeseburger..Cheeseburger

American Bacon-Cheeseburgers

1 (1 pound) package bacon 5 kg	Lettuce
2 pounds ground beef 1 kg	Tomatoes
8 slices cheese	Pickle slices
8 hamburger buns	Mustard/Mayonnaise
1 large onion, sliced	Ketchup

- Fry bacon and drain drippings from pan. Mix ground beef, salt and pepper and form into 8 patties. Cook on charcoal grill or in skillet until almost done. Add cheese slice on top of meat.
- Allow cheese to melt and put meat on warm bun. Add bacon, onions, lettuce, tomatoes and pickles. Dress with mustard, mayonnaise and/or ketchup.

■

California Burgers

- Replace ground beef with ground turkey. Use bean sprouts, avocado slices and tomatoes instead of bacon, onions, lettuce and pickles.

■

Western Burgers

- Replace raw onion with sauteed onion, sauteed fresh mushrooms and add chili sauce, hickory sauce or ketchup.

■

Southwestern Burgers

- Use green chili salsa and grated Mexican, four-cheese blend.

■ ■ ■

Strike Up The Band

Jack's Firecrackers

1¼ pounds lean ground beef	567 g
1 (2 ounce) chunk Monterey Jack cheese with jalapeno peppers	57 g
4 hamburger buns	
Lettuce and tomatoes	

- Preheat grill or broiler to high. Evenly divide ground beef into 8 large flat patties. Cut cheese into 4 cubes.
- Place 1 piece of cheese on top of each 4 pattics, top with remaining 4 patties and press edges lightly to seal.
- Place burgers in broiler pan and broil or grill 8 to 10 minutes on each side. Serve on hamburger buns with lettuce and tomatoes.

TIP: This is also great with crumbled blue cheese.

■

Avocado-Corn Salad

2 ripe avocados, peeled, diced	
2 tablespoons fresh lime juice	30 ml
3 cups halved grape tomatoes	710 ml
2 (11 ounce) cans mexicorn, drained	2 (312 g*

- Place avocados in salad bowl and spoon lime juice and a little salt over avocados. Add tomatoes and corn. Spoon about ½ cup (120 ml) zesty Italian dressing over salad and serve.

Beefy Sandwiches

Roast Beef Sandwiches

2 - 2½ cups roast	480 ml
½ cup drained, sweet pickle relish	120 ml
3 celery ribs, chopped	
2 eggs, hard-boiled, chopped	
1 - 1½ cups mayonnaise	240 ml

- Place roast pieces in blender and pulse several times to chop roast.
- Add pickle relish, celery, eggs, 1 teaspoon (5 ml) each of salt and pepper and mix well. Stir in enough mayonnaise to blend roast-egg mixture.
- Spread on bread to make sandwiches or on crackers for snack.

■

Stompin' Good Jalapeno Squares

2 (4 ounce) cans jalapeno peppers, seeded, chopped	2 (114 g)
1 (1 pound) package bacon, fried, crumbled	.5 kg
1 (12 ounce) package shredded Mexican 4-cheese blend	340 g
1 (4 ounce) can sliced mushroom stems and pieces, drained	114 g
10 eggs, well beaten	

- Preheat oven to 325° (162 C). Line bottom of greased 9 x 13-inch (23 x 33 cm) baking dish with jalapenos.
- Sprinkle bacon pieces, cheese and mushrooms in layers. Pour beaten eggs over top.
- Cook for about 25 to 30 minutes or until center is firm. Let stand 15 minutes before slicing. Cut into squares and serve hot.

TIP: *If you want a mild "hot", just use 1 can jalapenos.*

■ ■ ■

Italian Night

Speedy Steak Stromboli

2 pounds frozen pizza dough, thawed	**1 kg**
⅔ cup hot salsa	**160 ml**
½ pound sliced roast beef	**227 g**
1 (8 ounce) package shredded cheddar cheese	**227 g**

- Preheat oven to 425° (220° C). On floured surface, roll out half the dough into 10 x 14-inch (25 x 36 cm) rectangle.
- Spread half salsa over dough and leave ½-inch (1.2 cm) border. Cover with half sliced roast beef and half cheese. Starting at long side, roll jellyroll-style and pinch ends together. Place on greased baking sheet.
- Repeat with remaining ingredients for second roll. Bake 20 minutes or until light brown. Cool about 20 minutes and slice to serve.

■

Tri-Color Pasta Salad

3 cups tri-color spiral pasta	**710 ml**
1 tablespoon olive oil	**15 ml**
1 (8 ounce) package shredded cheddar cheese	**227 g**
1 large bunch broccoli, cut into small florets	
1 cup chopped celery	**240 ml**
1 cup cubed cucumber	**240 ml**

- Cook pasta according to package directions, drain well and toss with olive oil to keep pasta from sticking together
- Transfer to large salad bowl and add cheese, broccoli, celery, cucumber and salt and pepper to taste.
- Toss with creamy ranch salad dressing.

■ ■ ■

Multiply Sandwiches

Reuben Sandwiches

For each sandwich:

2 slices rye bread	
1 slice Swiss cheese	
Generous slices corned beef	
2 tablespoons sauerkraut	30 ml
Thousand Island dressing	

- Butter 1 slice bread on 1 side. Place butter side down in skillet over low heat.
- Layer cheese, corned beef and sauerkraut on bread and spread dressing on 1 side of other slice. Butter opposite side of bread. Place butter side up on sauerkraut.
- Cook until bottom browns, turn carefully and brown other side.

■

Spicy Tomato Soup

2 (10 ounce) cans tomato soup	2 (280 g)
1 (16 ounce) can Mexican stewed tomatoes	.5 kg
Sour cream	
½ pound bacon, fried, drained, crumbled	227 g

- In saucepan, combine soup and stewed tomatoes and heat.
- To serve, place dollop of sour cream on each bowl of soup and sprinkle crumbled bacon over sour cream.

Hot Dog!

Top-Notch Hot Dogs

10 (8-inch) flour tortillas	10 (20 cm)
10 hot dogs	
1 (15 ounce) can chili with beans, warmed	425 g
1 (16 ounce) jar thick-and-chunky salsa	.5 kg
1 (8 ounce) package Mexican-style shredded cheese	227 g

- Preheat oven to 325° (162° C). Spray 9 x 13-inch (23 x 33 cm) baking dish. Soften tortillas according to package directions.
- Place 1 hot dog and 3 tablespoons (45 ml) chili on each tortilla and roll. Place seam-side down on baking dish. Pour salsa over tortillas. Cover with foil and bake 25 minutes. Uncover and sprinkle cheese over tortillas. Return to oven for 5 minutes.

■

Crunchy Potato Salad

10 - 12 small new red potatoes, cut in wedges	
1 (10 ounce) package red-tip lettuce	280 g
6 ounces feta cheese	168 g
½ cup pecan halves	120 ml
⅓ cup chopped onions	80 ml
¼ cup honey	60 ml
¼ cup lemon juice	60 ml
½ cup olive oil	120 ml
3 eggs, hard-boiled, cut in wedges	

- In saucepan, cook potatoes in salted water about 15 minutes or until tender. Drain and cool. In salad bowl, combine lettuce, crumbled feta cheese, pecans and onions.
- Combine honey, lemon juice and oil and mix well. Pour over salad and toss. Garnish with egg wedges.

■ ■ ■

Quick Meal From The Freezer

Hot Bunwiches

8 hamburger buns
8 slices Swiss cheese
8 slices ham
8 slices turkey
8 slices American cheese

- Lay out all 8 buns and place slices of Swiss cheese, ham, turkey and American cheese on bottom buns.
- Place top bun over American cheese, wrap each bunwich individually in foil and place in freezer. Remove from freezer 2 to 3 hours before serving.
- Heat at 325° (162° C) for about 30 minutes and serve hot.

■

Stained-Glass Fruit Salad

2 (20 ounce) cans peach pie filling	**2 (567 g)**
3 bananas, sliced	
1 (16 ounce) package frozen unsweetened	
strawberries, drained	**.5 kg**
1 (20 ounce) can pineapple tidbits, drained	**567 g**

- Mix fruits, chill and place in pretty crystal bowl. Chill overnight.

■ ■ ■

"You'll Never Guess" Sandwich

Turkey Surprise

1 pound deli-shaved smoked turkey slices	.5 kg
1 (8 ounce) package provolone cheese slices	227 g
2 - 3 avocados	
2 green apples	
1 (24 ounce) loaf oatnut bread or whole wheat bread	680 g

- To make 6 sandwiches, place 6 slices bread on counter and spread very slight amount of mayonnaise on each slice.
- Place several pieces of turkey on each slice of bread and layer provolone cheese and several slices avocado with dash salt.
- Now for the surprise! Peel and core apples and with your very best knife, cut very, very thin slices of apple and place over avocado.
- Spread mayonnaise on 6 more slices bread and top sandwich with remaining bread.

■

Bacon-Potato Soup

2 (14 ounce) cans chicken broth seasoned with garlic	2 (396 g)
2 potatoes, peeled, cubed	
1 onion, finely chopped	
6 slices bacon, cooked, crumbled	

- In large saucepan, combine broth, potatoes and onion. Bring to a boil, reduce heat to medium high and boil about 10 minutes or until potatoes are tender. Season with pepper. Ladle into bowls and sprinkle with crumbled bacon.

New Sandwich Night

Turkey-Asparagus Sandwiches

4 (1 ounce) slices cheddar cheese	4 (28 g)
2 English muffins, split, toasted	
½ pound thinly sliced turkey	227 g
1 (15 ounce) can asparagus spears, drained	425 g
1 (1 ounce) package hollandaise sauce blend	28 g

- Place 1 cheese slice on each muffin half and top evenly with turkey.
- Cut asparagus spears to fit muffin halves and top each with 3 or 4 asparagus spears. (Reserve remaining asparagus for another use.)
- Prepare hollandaise sauce mix according to package directions, pour evenly over sandwiches and sprinkle with paprika, if desired.

■

Cherry-Cranberry Salad

1 (6 ounce) package cherry gelatin	168 g
1 (20 ounce) can cherry pie filling	567 g
1 (16 ounce) can whole cranberry sauce	.5 kg

- In mixing bowl, combine cherry gelatin and 1 cup (240 ml) boiling water and mix until gelatin dissolves.
- Mix pie filling and cranberry sauce into gelatin. Pour into 7 x 11-inch (18 x 28 cm) dish and refrigerate.

Perfect Leftover Turkey Sandwich

Turkey-Cranberry Croissant

1 (8 ounce) package cream cheese, softened	227 g
¼ cup orange marmalade	60 ml
6 large croissants, split	
Lettuce leaves	
1 pound thinly sliced, cooked turkey	.5 kg
¾ cup whole berry cranberry sauce	180 ml

- Beat cream cheese and orange marmalade and spread evenly on cut sides of croissants.
- Place lettuce leaves and turkey on croissant bottoms and spread with cranberry sauce. Cover with croissant tops and serve.

■

Cherry Crush

1 (6 ounce) box cherry gelatin	168 g
1 (8 ounce) package cream cheese, softened	227 g
1 (20 ounce) can cherry pie filling	567 g
1 (15 ounce) can crushed pineapple with juice	425 g

- Dissolve gelatin with ¾ cup (180 ml) boiling water. With electric mixer beat in cream cheese very slowly at first.
- Fold in pie filling and crushed pineapple. Pour into 9 x 13-inch (23 x 33 cm) baking dish. Refrigerate.

■ ■ ■

Reward for All

Honey-Do Reward Sandwich

1 (16 ounce) jar refrigerated honey-mustard dressing	.5 kg
4 kaiser rolls, split	
8 thin slices honey ham	
8 slices Swiss cheese	

- Preheat oven to 400° (204° C). Spread honey-mustard on each split roll. (You will not need all of dressing.) Top each with ham and cheese slices. Place on baking sheet and bake 4 to 5 minutes or until cheese melts.

■

Sesame-Broccoli Salad

1 (16 ounce) package broccoli-rabe slaw	.5 kg
1 sweet red bell pepper, seeded, chopped	
2 (9 ounce) packages fresh tortellini, cooked	2 (255 g)
1 (8 ounce) bottle vinaigrette salad dressing	227 g
2 tablespoons olive oil	30 ml
¼ cup sesame seeds, toasted	60 ml

- In salad bowl, combine broccoli-rabe, bell pepper and cooked tortellini. Drizzle salad dressing and olive oil over salad and toss. Chill and just before serving, sprinkle sesame seeds over salad.

TIP: *Toasting bring out the flavors of nuts and seeds. Place nut or seeds on baking sheet and bake at 225° (107° C) for 10 minutes. Be careful not to burn them.*

It Starts Out Big

EDITORS CHOICE

Big-Time Family Sandwich

1 (11 ounce) bottle dijon-style gourmayo	312 g
1 (16 ounce) loaf French bread, halved	.5 kg
8 slices Swiss cheese	
8 slices honey ham	
16 dill pickle sandwich slices	

- Preheat oven to 375° (190° C). Spread dijon-style gourmayo over cut sides of bread. Arrange half of cheese and half of ham on bottom slice and top with pickle slices. Spread remaining cheese and ham on top of pickles.

- Cover with top of bread, press down on sandwich and cut into quarters. Place on baking sheet and bake for 5 minutes and serve immediately.

■

Zesty Fruit Salad

1 (24 ounce) jar refrigerated mixed fruit salad, drained	680 g
1 (24 ounce) jar refrigerated red grapefruit, drained	680 g
1 red delicious apple, unpeeled, thinly sliced	
¼ cup slivered almonds, toasted	

Dressing:

⅔ cup honey	160 ml
¼ cup frozen limeade concentrate, thawed	60 ml
2 teaspoons poppy seeds	10 ml

- In salad bowl, combine all fruits. In small bowl, combine honey, limeade concentrate and poppy seeds and toss with fruit. Sprinkle with almonds.

■ ■ ■

Seafood Burgers

Salmon Burgers

1 (15 ounce) can salmon with liquid	425 g
1 egg, slightly beaten	
¼ cup lemon juice	60 ml
⅔ cup seasoned breadcrumbs	160 ml
Hamburger buns	
Mayonnaise	
Lettuce	
Sliced tomatoes	

- In bowl, combine salmon, 2 tablespoons (30 ml) salmon liquid, egg, lemon juice, breadcrumbs and salt and pepper to taste. Form into patties and cook in a little oil on both sides until golden.
- Serve hot on buns with mayonnaise, lettuce and sliced tomatoes.

■

Fiesta-Vegetable Soup

1 (15 ounce) can Mexican-style stewed tomatoes	425 g
1 (15 ounce) can whole kernel corn	425 g
1 (15 ounce) can pinto beans	425 g
2 (14 ounce) cans chicken broth	2 (396 g)
1 (10 ounce) can fiesta nacho soup	280 g

- In soup pot over high heat, combine tomatoes, corn, pinto beans, chicken broth and salt to taste and mix well. Stir in fiesta nacho soup and heat just until thoroughly hot.

MAIN DISH MEALS

Sundae Night Treat

Skillet Nachos

½ (16 ounce) package tortilla chips	½ (.5 kg)
1 (8 ounce) can whole kernel corn, drained	227 g
1 cup chili beans	240 ml
¾ cup thick-and-chunky salsa, divided	180 ml
1 (8 ounce) package shredded 4-cheese blend	227 g
1 (4 ounce) can sliced ripe olives	114 g

- Arrange tortilla chips in single layer in large 12-inch (32 cm) skillet. (Use skillet you can take to the table.) In saucepan, combine corn, beans and ½ cup (120 ml) salsa and heat just until hot and bubbly.

" Spoon salsa mixture over tortilla chips, then sprinkle on about three-fourths of cheese. Cover skillet and cook on medium-high heat for about 5 minutes or until cheese melts. To serve, sprinkle ripe olives and remaining cheese over top. You may want to serve with more salsa.

■

Chocolate Cookie Sundae

½ cup (1 stick) butter	120 ml
1 (19 ounce) package chocolate sandwich cookies, crushed	538 g
½ gallon vanilla ice cream, softened	2 L
2 (12 ounce) jars fudge sauce	2 (340 g)
1 (12 ounce) carton whipped topping	340 g

" Melt butter in 9 x 13-inch (23 x 33 cm) pan. Reserve about ½ cup (120 ml) crushed cookies for topping and mix remaining crumbs with butter to form crust. Press crumb mixture into pan.

" Spread softened ice cream over crust (work fast) and add fudge sauce on top. Top with whipped topping and sprinkle with remaining crumbs. Freeze.

■ ■ ■

Amigo Night

Border Taco Pie

1 pound lean ground beef	.5 kg
½ bell pepper and jalapeno pepper, seeded, chopped	
1 (15 ounce) can Mexican stewed tomatoes	425 g
1 tablespoon chili powder	15 ml
8 ounces shredded sharp cheddar cheese	227 g
1 (8 ounce) package corn muffin mix	227 g
1 egg	
⅓ cup milk	80 ml

- Brown ground beef, bell pepper and jalapeno peppers in a little oil in large skillet and drain well. Add salt to taste, tomatoes, 1 cup (240 ml) water and chili powder. Cook on medium heat for about 10 minutes or until most liquid cooks out.

- Pour into greased 9 x 13-inch (23 x 33 cm) glass-baking dish. Sprinkle cheese on top.

- Combine muffin mix, egg and milk; beat well. Pour over top of cheese. Bake at 375° (190° C) for 25 minutes or until muffin mix is light brown. Set aside about 10 minutes before serving.

■

Surprise Chocolates

2 pounds white chocolate or almond bark	1 kg
2 cups Spanish peanuts	480 ml
2 cups small pretzel sticks, broken	480 ml

- Melt chocolate in double boiler. Stir in peanuts and pretzels. Drop by teaspoonfuls onto wax paper. Work fast because mixture hardens quickly.

- Place in freezer for 1 hour before storing at room temperature.

■ ■ ■

Terrific Quick Dish

Chili Casserole

1 (40 ounce) can chili with beans	1.1 kg
1 (4 ounce) can chopped green chilies	114 g
1 (2 ounce) can sliced ripe olives, drained	57 g
1 (8 ounce) package shredded cheddar cheese	227 g
2 cups crushed ranch-flavored tortilla chips	480 ml

- Combine all ingredients and transfer to greased 3-quart (3 L) baking dish.
- Bake uncovered at 350° (176° C) for 35 minutes or until bubbly.

■

Marinated Cucumbers

3 cucumbers, thinly sliced	
2 (4 ounce) jars chopped pimentos, drained	2 (114 g)
⅔ cup oil	160 ml
¼ cup white wine vinegar	60 ml
1 (8 ounce) carton sour cream	227 g

- Mix cucumber and pimentos. Combine oil, vinegar and ½ teaspoon (2 ml) salt. Pour over cucumbers and chill 1 hour.
- To serve, drain well and pour sour cream over cucumbers and pimentos and toss.

Quick Sunday-Night Supper

2 (15 ounce) cans chili without beans	2 (425 g)
2 (15 ounce) cans pinto beans with juice	2 (425 g)
2 (15 ounce) cans beef tamales without shucks	2 (425 g)
1 (8 ounce) package shredded Mexican 4-cheese blend, divided	227 g

- Preheat oven to 350° (176° C). In greased 9 x 13-inch (23 x 33 cm) baking pan, spoon both cans chili in pan and spread out with back of large spoon.

- Spread beans with juice over chili. Spread tamales over beans. Sprinkle about ½ cup (120 ml) cheese over top, cover and bake 30 minutes.

- Remove from oven and sprinkle remaining cheese over top of casserole. Return to oven for just 5 minutes. Serve with lots of tortilla chips.

TIP: *You might want to serve some hot thick, chunky salsa along with this dish.*

■

Toasted French Bread

1 unsliced loaf French bread	
½ cup (1 stick) butter, softened	120 ml
¾ cup parmesan cheese	180 ml
1½ teaspoons hot sauce	7 ml

- Slice bread in half lengthwise, then quarter. Combine butter, parmesan cheese and hot sauce. Spread on top of slices using all of mixture.

- Place on baking sheet and cook at 325° (162° C) for about 25 minutes or until thoroughly hot.

Quick Mexi-Fix

Corny Chili and Beans

2 (15 ounce) cans chili with beans	2 (425 g)
1 (15 ounce) can Mexican-style stewed tomatoes	425 g
1 (11 ounce) can mexicorn, drained	312 g
2 diced ripe avocados	

- Combine chili, tomatoes and corn in microwave-safe bowl. Cover loosely and cook on high in microwave for about 4 minutes.
- Stir in diced avocados and serve hot.

■

Green Chili and Cheese Bread

1 loaf unsliced Italian bread	
½ cup (1 stick) butter, melted	120 ml
1 (4 ounce) can diced green chilies, drained	114 g
¾ cup grated Monterey Jack cheese	180 ml

- Slice bread almost all the way through. Combine melted butter, chilies and cheese. Spread between bread slices.
- Cover loaf with foil and bake at 350° (176° C) for 25 minutes.

Pinto Beef Pie

1 pound lean ground beef	.5 kg
1 onion, chopped	
2 (16 ounce) cans pinto beans with liquid	2 (.5 kg)
1 (10 ounce) can tomatoes and green chilies with liquid	280 g
1 (6 ounce) can french-fried onion rings	168 g

- In skillet, brown beef and onion and drain.
- In 2-quart (2 L) baking dish, layer 1 can beans, beef-onion mixture and ½ can tomatoes and green chilies. Repeat layer.
- Top with onion rings and bake uncovered at 350° (176° C) for 30 minutes.

■

Red and Green Salad

2 (10 ounce) packages fresh spinach	2 (280 g)
1 quart fresh strawberries, halved	1 L
½ cup slivered almonds, toasted	120 ml
Poppy seed salad dressing	

- Tear spinach into small pieces and add strawberries and almonds.
- Refrigerate until ready to serve. Toss with poppy seed dressing.

■ ■ ■

Beefy Good and Sundaes

Taco Bueno Bake

2 pounds ground beef	1 kg
1½ cups taco sauce	360 ml
2 (15 ounce) cans Spanish rice	2 (425 g)
1 (8 ounce) package shredded Mexican 4-cheese blend, divided	227 g

- Brown ground beef in skillet and drain. Add taco sauce, rice and half cheese. Spoon mixture into buttered 3-quart (3 L) baking dish.
- Cover and bake at 350° (176° C) for 35 minutes. Uncover and sprinkle remaining cheese on top and return to oven for 5 minutes.

■

Peanut Butter Sundaes

1 cup light corn syrup	240 ml
1 cup chunky peanut butter	240 ml
¼ cup milk	60 ml
Ice cream or pound cake	

- Stir corn syrup, peanut butter and milk in mixing bowl until they blend well. Serve over ice cream or pound cake.

Super-Duper Supper

Beef and Potato Mix

2 pounds lean ground beef	1 kg
1 onion, chopped	
1 (2 pound) package frozen tater tots	1 kg
1 (8 ounce) package shredded cheddar cheese	227 g
2 (10 ounce) cans cream of mushroom soup	2 (280 g)
1 soup can milk	

- Crumble uncooked ground beef into sprayed 9 x 13-inch (23 x 33 cm) glass baking dish. Sprinkle with a little salt and pepper.
- Cover with chopped onion. Top with tater tots and sprinkle cheese. Combine soups and milk in saucepan. Heat and stir just enough to mix in milk. Pour over casserole.
- Bake covered at 350° (176° C) for 1 hour. Uncover and bake another 15 minutes.

■

Lemon Cookies

½ cup (1 stick) butter, softened	120 ml
1 cup sugar	240 ml
2 tablespoons lemon juice	30 ml
2 cups flour	480 ml

- Cream butter, sugar and lemon juice and slowly stir in flour. Drop by teaspoons onto ungreased cookie sheet. Bake at 350° (176° C) for 14 to 15 minutes.

Pass The Plate

EDITORS
CHOICE

Easy Meat 'N Potatoes

1 pound ground beef	.5 kg
1 (10 ounce) can sloppy Joe sauce	280 g
1 (10 ounce) can fiesta nacho cheese soup	280 g
1 (32 ounce) package frozen hash brown potatoes, thawed	1 kg

- Brown beef in skillet over medium heat and drain. Add sloppy Joe sauce and fiesta nacho cheese soup to beef and mix well.
- Place hash browns in greased 9 x 13-inch (23 x 33 cm) baking dish and top with beef mixture. Cover and bake at 400° (204°) for 25 minutes. Uncover and bake 10 minutes longer.

TIP: *This is really good sprinkled with 1 cup (240 ml) grated cheddar cheese.*

■

Carrot Salad

3 cups finely grated carrots	710 ml
1 (8 ounce) can crushed pineapple, drained	227 g
4 tablespoons flaked coconut	60 ml
1 tablespoon sugar	15 ml
⅓ cup mayonnaise	80 ml

- Combine all ingredients. Mix well and refrigerate.

■ ■ ■

In Your Face Delicious

Smothered Beef Patties

1½ pounds lean ground beef	680 g
½ cup chili sauce	120 ml
½ cup buttery cracker crumbs	120 ml
1 (14 ounce) can beef bouillon	396 g

- Combine beef, chili sauce and cracker crumbs and form into 5 or 6 patties. In skillet, brown patties and pour beef bouillon over top.
- Bring to boil. Reduce heat, cover and simmer for about 40 minutes.

■

Asparagus Bake

4 (10 ounce) cans asparagus	4 (280 g)
3 eggs, hard-boiled, sliced	
⅓ cup milk	80 ml
1½ cups grated cheddar cheese	360 ml
1¼ cups cheese-cracker crumbs	300 ml

- Place asparagus in 7 x 11-inch (18 x 28 cm) baking dish, layer hard-boiled eggs on top and pour milk over casserole.
- Sprinkle cheese on top and add cracker crumbs. Bake uncovered at 350° (176° C) for 30 minutes.

■ ■ ■

Just the Basics

Potato-Beef Casserole

4 medium potatoes, peeled, sliced	
1¼ pounds lean ground beef, browned, drained	567 g
1 (10 ounce) can cream of mushroom soup	280 ml
1 (10 ounce) can condensed vegetable beef soup	280 ml

- In large bowl, combine all ingredients. Add a little salt and pepper to taste. Transfer to greased 3-quart (3 L) baking dish.
- Bake covered at 350° (176° C) for 1 hour 30 minutes or until potatoes are tender.

■

Special Spinach Salad

1 (10 ounce) package fresh spinach	280 g
1 (16 ounce) can bean sprouts, drained	.5 kg
8 slices bacon, cooked crisp, crumbled	
1 (11 ounce) can water chestnuts, chopped	312 g

- Combine spinach and bean sprouts. When ready to serve add crumbled bacon and toss with vinaigrette salad dressing.

TIP: *If you don't have vinaigrette on hand, you can make it with 3 parts olive oil and 1 part red wine vinegar.*

■ ■ ■

Lickety Skillet

Quick Skillet

1½ pounds lean ground beef	.7 kg
⅔ cup stir-fry sauce	160 ml
1 (16 ounce) package frozen stir-fry vegetables	.5 kg
2 (3 ounce) packages Oriental-flavor ramen noodles	2 (84 g)

- Brown and crumble ground beef in large skillet. Add 2½ cups (600 ml) water, stir-fry sauce to taste, vegetables and seasoning packets with ramen noodles.
- Cook and stir on low to medium heat about 5 minutes.
- Break noodles, add to beef-vegetable mixture and cook about 6 minutes. Stir to separate noodles as they soften.

■

Cashew Pea Salad

1 (16 ounce) package frozen green peas, thawed	.5 kg
¼ cup diced celery	60 ml
1 bunch fresh green onions with tops, chopped	
1 cup chopped cashews	240 ml
½ cup mayonnaise	120 ml

- Combine peas, celery, onions and cashews. Toss with mayonnaise and a little salt and pepper.

■ ■ ■

Cold Winter's Night

Winter Chili Supper

1 (40 ounce) can chili with beans	1.1 kg
1 (7 ounce) can chopped green chilies	198 g
1 bunch fresh green onions, sliced	
1 (8 ounce) package shredded Mexican 4-cheese blend	227 g
2½ cups crushed ranch-flavored tortilla chips, divided	600 ml

- Preheat oven to 350° (176° C). Combine chili, green chilies, onions, cheese and 2 cups (480 ml) crushed chips. Transfer to sprayed 3-quart (3 L) baking dish and bake 25 minutes.
- Remove from oven and sprinkle remaining chips over top of casserole and bake another 10 minutes.

■

Spiced-Up The Macaroni

1 (8 ounce) package spiral pasta	227 g
⅓ cup (5½ tablespoons) butter	80 ml
1 (8 ounce) package Mexican processed cheese	227 g
1 (10 ounce) can tomatoes and green chilies with liquid	280 g
½ yellow onion, very finely diced	
1 (8 ounce) carton sour cream	227 g

- Cook macaroni according to package directions and drain. Add butter and stir continuously until butter melts. Set aside, covered and keep warm
- Preheat oven to 325° (162° C). In large saucepan, combine processed cheese, tomatoes and green chilies and diced onion. Stir in macaroni and heat on low for 5 minutes, stir occasionally.
- Fold in sour cream and pour into 2-quart (2 L) baking dish. Cover and bake for 20 minutes.

■ ■ ■

All-Around Good Meal

Potato-Beef Casserole

4 medium potatoes, peeled, sliced
1¼ pounds lean ground beef, browned, drained   567 g
1 (10 ounce) can cream of mushroom soup   280 g
1 (10 ounce) can condensed vegetable beef soup   280 g

- In large bowl, combine all ingredients plus ½ teaspoon (2 ml) each of salt and pepper and transfer to greased 3-quart (3 L) baking dish.
- Bake covered at 350° (176° C) for 1 hour 30 minutes or until potatoes are tender.

■

Orange-Almond Salad

1 head green leaf lettuce
4 slices bacon, fried, crumbled
⅓ cup slivered almonds, toasted   80 ml
1 (11 ounce) can mandarin oranges, drained,
    chilled   312 g

- Combine all ingredients in salad bowl. When ready to serve toss with vinaigrette dressing.

■ ■ ■

Nothing Fancy

Simple Casserole Supper

1 pound lean ground beef	.5 kg
¼ cup uncooked white rice	60 ml
1 (10 ounce) can French-onion soup	280 g
1 (6 ounce) can french-fried onion rings	168 g

- Brown ground beef, drain and place in buttered 7 x 11-inch (18 x 30 cm) baking dish. Add rice, onion soup and ½ cup (120 ml) water.
- Cover and bake at 325° (162° C) for 40 minutes. Uncover, sprinkle onion rings over top and return to oven for 10 minutes.

■

Salad Surprise

1 (10 ounce) bag fresh spinach, stemmed	280 g
1 pint fresh strawberries, stemmed, halved	.5 kg
1 large banana, sliced	
⅔ cup chopped walnuts	160 ml
Poppy seed dressing	

- Place all salad ingredients in large bowl. When ready to serve, toss with poppy seed dressing.

■ ■ ■

Muy Bien Amigos!

Bueno Taco Casserole

2 pounds lean ground beef	1 kg
1½ cups taco sauce	360 ml
2 (15 ounce) cans Spanish rice	2 (425 g)
1 (8 ounce) package shredded Mexican 4-cheese blend, divided	227 g

- In skillet, brown ground beef and drain. Add taco sauce, Spanish rice and half cheese. Spoon into buttered 3-quart (3 L) baking dish.
- Cover and bake at 350° (176° C) for 35 minutes. Uncover and sprinkle remaining cheese on top and return to oven for 5 minutes.

■

Ranch-French Bread

1 loaf unsliced French bread	
½ cup (1 stick) butter, softened	120 ml
1 tablespoon ranch-style dressing mix	15 ml
1 tablespoon mayonnaise, optional	15 ml

- Cut loaf in half horizontally. Blend butter and dressing mix.
- Spread butter mixture on bread. Wrap bread in foil. Bake at 350° (176° C) for 15 minutes.

Best-Ever Meatloaf

2 pounds lean ground beef	1 kg
¾ cup Italian-seasoned dry breadcrumbs	180 ml
2 large eggs, beaten	
2 (10 ounce) cans golden cream of mushroom soup, divided	2 (280 g)
¼ cup (½ stick) butter	60 ml
1¼ cups milk	300 ml

- Preheat oven to 350° (176° C). Mix beef, breadcrumbs, eggs and ½ can soup. In sprayed baking pan, shape firmly into 9 x 4-inch (23 x 10 cm) loaf and bake 45 minutes. Let stand about 10 minutes before slicing.

- In saucepan, combine remaining soup, butter and milk, mix well and heat, stirring often, until sauce is thoroughly hot. Serve over slices of meat loaf.

■

Sour Cream Biscuits

2 cups, plus 1 tablespoon flour	480 ml/15 ml
3 teaspoons baking powder	15 ml
½ teaspoon baking soda	2 ml
½ cup shortening	120 ml
1 (8 ounce) carton sour cream	227 g

- Preheat oven to 400° (204° C). Combine dry ingredients and add a little salt. Cut in shortening. Gradually add sour cream and mix lightly. Turn on lightly floured board and knead a few times.

- Roll to ½-inch (1.2 cm) thick. Cut with biscuit cutter and place on sprayed baking sheet. Bake 15 minutes or until light brown.

Skillet Supper

Beef Skillet Supper

1 pound lean ground beef	.5 kg
1 (10 ounce) can tomato soup	280 g
1 cup hot, chunky salsa	240 ml
6 (6-inch) flour tortillas, cut into 1-inch/2.5 cm pieces	6 (15 cm)
1½ cups shredded cheddar cheese	360 ml

- Brown and cook ground beef on medium-high heat in large, heavy skillet. Add soup, salsa, ¾ cup (180 ml) water, tortillas, salt to taste and half cheese; mix well.
- Cover and cook over low heat for 15 minutes. Top with remaining cheese and serve right from skillet.

■

Carrot-Apple Salad

1 (16 ounce) package shredded carrots	.5 kg
1 green and 1 red apple with peel, chopped	
½ cup golden raisins	120 ml
1 tablespoon mayonnaise	15 ml
1 tablespoon lemon juice	15 ml

- In bowl, combine shredded carrots, chopped apples and raisins. Add mayonnaise and lemon juice. Toss and refrigerate.

■ ■ ■

Time To Eat

It's-Time-To-Eat

1 pound lean ground beef	.5 kg
1 onion, chopped	
4 tablespoons steak sauce	60 ml
1 tablespoon flour	15 ml
1 (15 ounce) can baked beans with liquid	425 g
1 (8 ounce) can whole kernel corn, drained	227 g
1½ cups crushed garlic-flavored croutons	360 ml

- Preheat oven to 325° (162° C). Brown beef and onion in large skillet and drain. Stir in all remaining ingredients except croutons.
- Pour into sprayed 9 x 13-inch (23 x 33 cm) baking dish and sprinkle crouton crumbs on top. Bake uncovered for 45 minutes or until bubbly around edges.

■

Mandarin Fluff

2 (11 ounce) cans mandarin oranges, well drained	2 (312 g)
1 (14 ounce) can pineapple tidbits, well drained	396 g
1 cup miniature marshmallows	240 ml
1 (8 ounce) carton whipping topping	227 g
½ cup chopped pecans	120 ml

- Place oranges and pineapple in bowl and stir in marshmallows. (Make sure marshmallows are not stuck together.) Fold in whipped topping and pecans and chill. Serve in individual sherbet glasses.

Sleepy Night Treat

Good Night Casserole Supper

1 pound lean ground beef	.5 kg
1 onion, chopped	
1 red and 1 green pepper, seeded, chopped	
2 (10 ounce) cans golden cream of mushroom soup	2 (280 g)
⅔ cup uncooked white rice	160 ml
4 tablespoons soy sauce	60 ml
1 (3 ounce) can french-fried onion rings	84 g

- Preheat oven to 350° (176° C). Brown beef and onions in large skillet and drain. Pour into sprayed 9 x 13-inch (23 x 33 cm) baking dish.
- Stir in both bell peppers, both cans soup, rice, soy sauce, ¾ cup (180 ml) water, salt and pepper to taste. With paper towel, clean off edges of casserole dish and cover with foil.
- Bake for 45 minutes, remove dish from oven and sprinkle onion rings over top. Return to oven for 15 minutes.

Wilted Spinach Salad

1 (10 ounce) package fresh baby spinach	280 g
1 (15 ounce) can cannellini beans, rinsed, drained	425 g
¾ cup zesty Italian salad dressing	180 ml
¾ cup shredded Monterey Jack cheese	180 ml

- Remove large stems from spinach and place in salad bowl. Add cannellini beans and toss. In saucepan, heat Italian salad dressing to a boil, pour over spinach-bean mixture and toss.
- Sprinkle cheese over salad and serve immediately.

Luck Of The Irish

O'Brian's Hash

3 cups cubed, cooked beef roast	710 ml
1 (28 ounce) package frozen hash browns with onions and peppers, thawed	794 g
1 (16 ounce) jar salsa	.5 kg
1 tablespoon beef seasoning	15 ml
1 cup shredded cheddar-jack cheese	240 ml

- Place cubed beef in large slow cooker sprayed with vegetable cooking spray.
- Brown potatoes in little oil in large skillet and transfer to slow cooker. Stir in salsa and beef seasoning.
- Cover and cook on HIGH for 4 to 5 hours. When ready to serve, sprinkle cheese over hash.

■

Caramel-Apple Delight

3 (2 ounce) Snickers candy bars, frozen	3 (57 g)
2 Granny Smith apples, chopped	
1 (12 ounce) carton whipped topping	340 g
1 (3 ounce) package dry instant vanilla pudding	84 g

- Smash frozen candy bars in wrappers with hammer. Mix all ingredients together and chill.

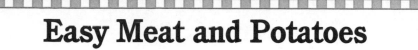

Easy Meat and Potatoes

Steak and Potatoes

2 pounds round steak	1 kg
⅓ cup flour	80 ml
⅓ cup oil	80 ml
5 potatoes, peeled, diced	
¼ cup chopped onions	60 ml
1 (10 ounce) cream of mushroom soup	280 g

- Preheat oven to 350° (176° C). Dice steak, coat in flour, brown in heavy skillet and drain. Place steak in 9-inch (23 cm) baking dish.
- Season potatoes with a little salt and pepper, place over steak and cover with mushroom soup diluted with ½ cup (120 ml) water. Bake 1 hour 30 minutes.

■

Mandarin Salad

1 head red-tipped lettuce	
2 (11 ounce) cans mandarin oranges, drained	2 (312 g)
2 avocadoes, peeled, diced	
1 small red onion, sliced	
Poppy seed dressing	

- Combine all ingredients. When ready to serve, toss with poppy seed dressing.

■ ■ ■

Corny Steak and Fun

Steak For Supper

1 pound round steak, cut in strips	.5 kg
1 (14 ounce) can beef broth	396 g
3 tablespoons cornstarch	45 ml
1 tablespoon soy sauce	15 ml
1 red and 1 green bell pepper, julienned	
1 (4.6 ounce) broccoli and cheese boil-in-bag rice mix	128 g

- In large skillet brown steak strips and reduce heat. Add ? cup (80 ml) water, cover and simmer until liquid evaporates.

- Combine beef broth, cornstarch and soy sauce (and a little garlic powder if you like) and pour over steak strips. Add bell peppers and stir until mixture boils and thickens.

- Cook rice according to package directions and serve steak over rice.

■

Corny Green Beans

1 (16 ounce) package frozen green beans, thawed	.5 kg
1 (16 ounce) package whole kernel corn, thawed	.5 kg
1 (8 ounce) carton sour cream	227 g
1 (8 ounce) package shredded 4-cheese blend	227 g

Topping:

2 cups crushed round butter-flavored crackers	480 ml
2 tablespoons butter, melted	30 ml

- Preheat oven to 350° (176° C). In large bowl, combine drained green beans, corn, soup, sour cream, cheese and a little salt and mix well. Spoon into sprayed 9 x 13-inch (23 x 33 cm) baking dish.

- Combine cracker crumbs and melted butter and sprinkle over top of casserole. Bake uncovered for 30 minutes.

Protein For The Boys

On-the-Border Steak

½ teaspoon dry mustard	2 ml
2 tablespoons fajita seasoning	30 ml
1 teaspoon minced garlic	5 ml
1½ pounds flank steak	680 g

- Combine ½ teaspoon (2 ml) pepper, dry mustard, fajita seasoning and garlic. Rub flank steak with a little oil, sprinkle seasonings over steak and chill 4 to 6 hours.
- Grill steak on each side on covered grill 6 to 8 minutes on medium heat. Cut steak diagonally across grain into thin strips. Serve with hot salsa over hot cooked rice.

■

Sunday Night Supper Rice

2 cups cooked white rice	480 ml
1 onion, chopped	
¼ cup (½ stick) butter, melted	60 ml
1 (8 ounce) package shredded Mexican processed cheese	227 g

- Combine all ingredients and mix well. Spoon mixture into buttered 2-quart (2 L) baking dish. Bake covered at 325° (162° C) for 30 minutes.

Marinated Steak

Oregano-Marinated Steak

2 pounds (1-inch) thick London broil steak	1 kg (2.5 cm)
½ cup bottled Greek vinaigrette dressing	120 ml
1 tablespoon dried oregano	15 ml
1 teaspoon lemon juice	5 ml

- Dry steak with paper towels. Combine vinaigrette, oregano, lemon juice and ½ teaspoon (2 ml) pepper in large baggie. Add steak and press air out of bag. Seal and turn several times to distribute marinade well. Refrigerate 1 hour.

- Remove steak from marinade, discard marinade and grill about 5 inches (13 cm) from heat for about 15 minutes for rare to medium steak. Slice steak against grain.

■

Macaroni and Cheese Reward

2 cups uncooked macaroni	480 ml
2 cups milk	480 ml
¼ cup flour	60 ml
1 (16 ounce) package shredded sharp cheddarcheese	.5 kg
1 cup soft breadcrumbs	240 ml
¼ cup (½ stick) melted butter	60 ml

- Preheat oven to 350° (176° C). Cook macaroni according to package directions, drain and set aside. In jar with lid, combine milk, flour and ample amount of seasoned salt. Shake to mix well.

- In large bowl, combine macaroni, flour-milk mixture and cheese and mix well. Pour into sprayed 9 x 13-inch (23 x 33 cm) baking dish. Stir melted butter over breadcrumbs and toss. Sprinkle breadcrumbs over top. Cover and bake 35 minutes; remove cover and return to oven for 10 minutes.

■ ■ ■

1-Dish Select

Thai Beef, Noodles And Veggies

2 (4.4 ounce) packages Thai sesame noodles	2 (128 g)
1 pound sirloin steak, cut in strips	.5 g
1 (16 ounce) package frozen stir-fry vegetables, thawed	.5 g
½ cup chopped peanuts	120 ml

- Cook noodles according to package directions, remove from heat and cover. Season sirloin strips with a little salt and pepper.
- Brown half sirloin strips in a little oil in skillet and cook about 2 minutes. Remove from skillet and drain. Add remaining sirloin strips, brown in skillet with a little oil and cook about 2 minutes.
- In same skillet place vegetables and ½ cup (120 ml) water, cover and cook 5 minutes or until tender-crisp. Remove from heat, add steak strips and toss to mix. To serve, sprinkle with chopped peanuts.

■

Peanut Clusters

1 (24 ounce) package almond bark	680 g
1 (12 ounce) package milk chocolate chips	340 g
5 cups salted peanuts	1.3 L

- Melt almond bark and chocolate chips in double boiler. Stir in peanuts and drop by teaspoons onto wax paper.
- Place in refrigerator for 30 minutes to set. Store in airtight container.

Skillet Skill

Skillet Steak and Veggies

1 pound boneless sirloin steak, cut in strips	.5 kg
2 (15 ounce) cans Italian stewed tomatoes with juice	2 (425 g)
1 (16 ounce) package frozen Italian green beans, thawed	.5 kg
1 (8 ounce) carton sour cream	227 g

- Place sirloin strips in large skillet with a little oil. Cook on high heat about 3 minutes.
- Add stewed tomatoes and green beans, bring to boiling, lower heat and cook 5 minutes. Just before serving, fold in sour cream. Serve over hot, cooked egg noodles.

■

Ice Cream Dessert

19 ice cream sandwiches	
1 (12 ounce) carton whipped topping, thawed	340 g
1 (12 ounce) jar hot fudge ice cream topping	340 g
1 cup salted peanuts, divided	240 ml

- Cut 1 ice cream sandwich in half. Place 1 whole and 1 half sandwich along short side of ungreased 9 x 13-inch (23 x 33 cm) pan. Arrange 8 sandwiches in opposite direction in pan.
- Spread with half of whipped topping. Spoon fudge topping by teaspoonfuls onto whipped topping. Sprinkle with ½ cup (120 ml) peanuts.
- Repeat layers with remaining ice cream sandwiches, whipped topping and peanuts. (Pan will be full.) Cover and freeze. To serve, thaw for 20 minutes.

Beef Strips

Marinated Beef Strips

2 teaspoons oil	10 ml
2 teaspoons minced garlic	10 ml
½ teaspoon cayenne pepper	2 ml
2 tablespoons soy sauce	30 ml
2 tablespoons honey	30 ml
1 pound beef sirloin, thinly sliced	.5 kg

- Combine oil, garlic, cayenne pepper, soy sauce and honey and place in plastic freezer bag. Add sliced beef, seal and shake. Refrigerate for 30 minutes.
- Place beef slices in large sprayed skillet over medium-high heat and cook 5 to 6 minutes or until done.

■

Scalloped Potatoes

1 (4.9 ounce) box real scalloped potatoes	143 g
⅔ cup milk	160 ml
1 tablespoon butter	15 ml

- Cook according to package directions and serve with sirloin.

■

Wilted Spinach With Walnuts

2 (8 ounce) packages baby spinach	2 (227 g)
1 teaspoon prepared minced garlic	5 ml
2 tablespoons olive oil	30 ml
¼ cup walnut halves, toasted	60 ml

- In large skillet, saute spinach and garlic in hot oil on medium-high heat for 6 minutes or until spinach wilts.
- Sprinkle a little salt over spinach and toss with walnuts.

■ ■ ■

Chinese Eat-In

Stir-Fry Cashew Chicken

1 pound chicken tenders, cut into strips	.5 kg
1 (16 ounce) package frozen broccoli, cauliflower and carrots	.5 kg
1 (8 ounce) jar stir-fry sauce	227 g
⅓ cup cashew halves	80 ml
1 (12 ounce) package chow mein noodles	340 g

- Place a little oil and stir-fry chicken strips in 12-inch (32 cm) wok or skillet over high heat for about 4 minutes.

- Add vegetables and stir-fry another 4 minutes or until vegetables are tender. Stir in stir-fry sauce and cook just until mixture is hot. Serve over chow mein noodles.

■

Melon Boats

2 cantaloupes, chilled	
4 cups red and green seedless grapes, chilled	1 L
1 cup mayonnaise	240 ml
⅓ cup frozen orange juice concentrate, thawed	80 ml

- Prepare each melon in 6 lengthwise sections, remove seeds and peel. Place on separate salad plates on lettuce leaves.

- Heap grapes over and around the cantaloupe slices. Combine mayonnaise and juice concentrate and mix well. Ladle over fruit.

The Devil Made Me Do It

Chicken Super Supper

5 boneless, skinless chicken breast halves
5 slices onion
5 potatoes, peeled, quartered
1(10 ounce) can cream of celery soup　　　　　　**280 g**

- Place chicken breasts in 9 x 13-inch (23 x 33 cm) greased baking dish. Top chicken with onion slices and place potatoes around chicken.
- Heat soup with ¼ cup (60 ml) water just enough to pour soup over chicken and vegetables. Bake covered at 325° (162° C) for 1 hour 10 minutes.

■

Devil's Food Cookies

1 (18 ounce) devil's food cake mix　　　　　　**510 g**
½ cup oil　　　　　　**120 ml**
2 eggs
¾ cup chopped pecans　　　　　　**180 ml**

- Combine cake mix, oil, eggs and pecans in mixing bowl and mix well. Drop by teaspoons onto non-stick cookie sheet.
- Bake at 350° (176° C) for 10 to 12 minutes. Cool and remove to wire rack.

The Good Life

Jambalaya

1 (8 ounce) package jambalaya mix	227 g
1 (6 ounce) package frozen chicken breast strips, thawed	168 g
1 (11 ounce) can mexicorn	312 g
1 (2 ounce) can chopped black olives	57 g

- Combine jambalaya mix and 2¼ cups (540 ml) water in soup or large saucepan. Heat to boiling, reduce heat and cook slowly 5 minutes.

- Add chopped chicken, corn and black olives. Heat to boiling, reduce heat and simmer about 20 minutes.

TIP: *You could also add leftover ham or sausage and 1 tablespoon lemon juice to change it up some.*

TIP: *If you want to serve more than 5 people, just double the recipe.*

■

Apricot Bake

4 (15 ounce) cans apricot halves, drained	4 (425 g)
1 (16 ounce) box light brown sugar, divided	.5 kg
2 cups Ritz cracker crumbs, divided	480 ml
½ cup (1 stick) butter, sliced	120 ml

- Line bottom of greased, 9 x 13-inch (23 x 33 cm) baking dish with 2 cans of drained apricots. Sprinkle half brown sugar and half cracker crumbs over apricots.

- Dot with half butter. Repeat layers. Bake at 300° (148° C) for 1 hour.

There's Nothing Wrong With Broccoli

Broccoli-Cheese Chicken

1 tablespoon butter	15 ml
4 boneless, skinless chicken breast halves	
1 (10 ounce) can condensed broccoli-cheese soup	280 g
1 (10 ounce) package frozen broccoli spears	280 ml
⅓ cup milk	80 ml

- Heat butter in skillet, cook chicken 15 minutes or until brown on both sides, remove and set aside.
- In same skillet, combine soup, broccoli, milk and a little pepper and heat to boiling, return chicken to skillet and reduce heat to low.
- Cover, cook another 25 minutes until chicken is no longer pink and broccoli is tender and serve over rice.

■

Spiced Pears

1 (15 ounce) can pear halves	425 g
⅓ cup packed brown sugar	80 ml
¾ teaspoon ground nutmeg	4 ml
¾ teaspoon ground cinnamon	4 ml

- Drain pears and reserve syrup. Set pears aside. Place syrup, brown sugar, nutmeg and cinnamon in saucepan and bring to boil.
- Reduce heat and simmer uncovered for 5 to 8 minutes and stir often. Add pears and simmer 5 minutes longer or until it is thoroughly hot.

Ritzy Little Dish

Ritzy Chicken

6 boneless, skinless chicken breast halves

½ cup sour cream	**120 ml**
⅓ (12 ounce) box round buttery crackers, crushed	**⅓ 340 g**

- Dip chicken in sour cream and roll in ¼ teaspoon (1 ml) pepper mixed with cracker crumbs. Place chicken in greased, shallow baking dish.
- Bake uncovered at 350° (176° C) for 55 minutes.

■

Corn-Green Chili Casserole

2 (10 ounce) packages frozen whole kernel corn	**2 (280 g)**
2 tablespoons butter	**30 ml**
1 (8 ounce) package cream cheese	**227 g**
1 tablespoon sugar	**15 ml**
1 (4 ounce) can chopped green chilies	**114 g**

- Cook corn according to package directions, drain and set aside.
- Melt butter in saucepan over low heat, add cream cheese and stir until it melts. Stir in corn, sugar and green chilies. Spoon into greased 2-quart (2 L) baking dish.
- Cover and bake at 350° (176° C) for 25 minutes.

■ ■ ■

A Flash In The Pan

Fried Chicken Breasts

4 boneless, skinless chicken breast halves
20 saltine crackers, crushed
2 eggs, beaten

- Pound chicken breasts to ¼-inch (.6 cm) thickness. Combine eggs, ¼ teaspoon (1 ml) pepper and 2 tablespoons (30 ml) water.
- Dip chicken in egg mixture and crushed crackers and coat well. Deep fry until golden brown and drain well.

■

Broccoli Supreme

2 (10 ounce) packages broccoli spears	**2 (280 g)**
1 (6 ounce) roll garlic cheese	**168 g**
1 (10 ounce) can cream of mushroom soup	**280 g**
1 (3 ounce) can mushrooms, drained	**84 g**
¾ cup cornbread dressing mix, crushed	**180 ml**

- Boil broccoli for 3 minutes and drain. In saucepan, melt cheese on medium heat in mushroom soup. Add mushrooms and combine with broccoli.
- Pour broccoli mixture into greased 2-quart (2 L) baking dish and top with crushed cornbread dressing.
- Bake uncovered at 350° (176° C) for 30 minutes.

Chicken Hooray

Chicken Crunch

4 - 6 boneless, skinless chicken breast halves	
½ cup Italian salad dressing	120 ml
½ cup sour cream	120 ml
2½ cups crushed corn flakes	600 ml

- Place chicken in zip-top plastic bag and add salad dressing and sour cream. Seal and refrigerate 1 hour. Remove chicken from marinade and discard marinade.
- Dredge chicken in corn flakes and place in 9 x 13-inch (23 x 33 cm) non-stick sprayed baking dish.
- Bake uncovered at 375° (190° C) for 45 minutes.

■

Ranch Mashed Potatoes

4 cups prepared, unsalted instant mashed potatoes	1 L
1 (1 ounce) package dry ranch-style salad dressing mix	28 g
¼ cup (½ stick) butter	60 ml
½ cup sour cream	120 ml

- Combine all ingredients in saucepan and mix well. Heat on low until potatoes heat thoroughly.

Chicken Extraordinaire

Catalina Chicken

6 - 8 boneless, skinless chicken breast halves
1 (8 ounce) bottle Catalina dressing   **227 g**
1½ cups crushed cracker crumbs   **360 ml**

- Marinate chicken breasts in Catalina dressing for 3 to 4 hours and discard marinade. Combine 1 teaspoon (5 ml) pepper and cracker crumbs.
- Dip each chicken breast in crumbs and place in large, greased baking dish.
- Bake uncovered at 350° (176° C) for 1 hour.

■

Creamed Green Peas

1 (16 ounce) package frozen English peas   **.5 kg**
2 tablespoons (¼ stick) butter   **30 ml**
1 (10 ounce) can cream of celery soup   **280 g**
1 (3 ounce) package cream cheese   **84 g**
1 (8 ounce) can water chestnuts, drained   **227 g**

- Cook peas in microwave for 8 minutes and turn dish after 4 minutes.
- In large saucepan, combine butter, soup and cream cheese, cook on medium heat and stir until butter and cream cheese melt.
- Add peas and water chestnuts and mix. Serve hot.

Mexican Night

Chicken Casserole Pepe

1 (10 ounce) bag Doritos chips	280 g
1 onion, chopped	
1 (10 ounce) can cream of chicken soup	280 g
2 (10 ounce) can tomatoes and green chilies	2 (280 g)
1 (1 pound) box processed cheese, cubed	.5 kg
3 cups chopped chicken	710 ml

- Place half Doritos in sprayed 9 x 13-inch (23 x 33 cm) baking dish. Crush some with palm of hand.

- Combine onion, soup, tomatoes and green chilies and cheese in large saucepan. Heat on medium and stir until cheese melts. Add chicken and pour over Doritos.

- Crush remaining Doritos in baggie with rolling pin. Sprinkle over chicken-cheese mixture. Bake uncovered at 350° (176° C) for 40 minutes or until bubbly around edges.

■

Mexican Cornbread

1 (16 ounce) package Mexican cubed processed cheese	.5 kg
¼ cup milk	60 ml
2 (8 ounce) packages corn muffin mix	2 (227 g)
2 eggs, beaten	

- In saucepan, melt cheese with milk over low heat. Combine corn muffin mix and eggs in bowl. Fold in cheese and mix just until moist.

- Pour into greased 9 x 13-inch (23 x 33 cm) baking pan. Bake at 375° (190° C) for about 25 minutes or until light brown.

Enchilada Sunshine

Hurry-Up Chicken Enchiladas

2½ - 3 cups cooked, cubed chicken breasts	600 ml
1 (10 ounce) can cream of chicken soup	280 g
1½ cups chunky salsa, divided	360 ml
8 (6-inch) flour tortillas	8 (15 cm)
1 (10 ounce) can fiesta nacho cheese soup	280 g

- In saucepan, combine chicken, soup and ½ cup (120 ml) salsa and heat.
- Spoon about ⅓ cup (80 ml) chicken mixture down center of each tortilla and roll tortilla around filling. Place, seam-side down in sprayed 9 x 13-inch (23 x 33 cm) baking dish.
- Mix nacho cheese, remaining salsa and ¼ cup (60 ml) water and pour over enchiladas.
- Cover with wax paper and microwave on HIGH, turning several times, for 5 minutes or until bubbly.

■

Sunshine Salad

2 (15 ounce) cans mexicorn, drained	2 (425 g)
2 (15 ounce) cans peas, drained	2 (425 g)
1 (15 ounce) can kidney beans, rinsed, drained	425 g
1 (8 ounce) bottle Italian dressing	227 g

- Combine corn, peas and beans in large bowl. Pour salad dressing over vegetables and chill for several hours.

As The Chicken Flies

Chicken-Catch Casserole

3 cups cooked, chopped chicken or turkey	710 ml
1 (16 ounce) package frozen broccoli florets, thawed	.5 kg
1 (10 ounce) can cream of chicken soup, diluted	280 g
⅔ cup mayonnaise	160 ml
1 cup shredded cheddar cheese	240 ml
1½ cups crushed cheese crackers	360 ml

- Mix soup with ¼ cup (60 ml) water, combine with chicken, broccoli, mayonnaise and cheese and mix well.
- Pour into buttered 3-quart (3 L) baking dish and spread cheese crackers over top. Bake, uncovered, at 350° (176° C) for 40 minutes.

■

Green Beans With Tomatoes

2 pounds frozen, cut green beans	1 kg
4 tomatoes, chopped, drained	
1 bunch green onions, chopped	
1 cup Italian salad dressing	240 ml

- Place beans in saucepan, cover with water and bring to boil. Cook uncovered for 8 to 10 minutes or until tender crisp. Drain and chill.
- Add tomatoes, green onions and salad dressing and toss to coat.

■ ■ ■

Play It Again, Sam

Encore Chicken

6 boneless, skinless chicken breast halves
1 (16 ounce) jar thick, chunky hot salsa   .5 kg
1 cup packed light brown sugar   240 ml
1 tablespoon dijon-style mustard   15 ml

- Preheat oven to 325° (162° C).
- In large skillet with a little oil, brown chicken breasts and place in greased 9 x 13-inch (23 x 33 cm) baking dish.
- Combine salsa, brown sugar, mustard and ½ teaspoon (2 ml) salt and pour over chicken. Cover and bake 45 minutes. Serve over hot cooked brown rice.

■

Broccoli Salad

5 cups cut broccoli florets   1.3 L
1 red bell pepper, julienned
1 cup chopped celery   240 ml
8 - 12 ounces Monterey Jack cheese, cubed

- Combine all ingredients and mix well. Toss with Italian or your favorite dressing and refrigerate.

Pasta Night

Family-Night Spaghetti

6 frozen breaded, cooked chicken breast halves
1 (8 ounce) package spaghetti, cooked   **227 g**
1 (18 ounce) jar spaghetti sauce   **510 g**
1 (12 ounce) package shredded mozzarella cheese,
   divided   **340 g**

- Bake chicken breasts according to package directions and keep warm. Cook spaghetti according to package directions, drain and arrange on platter.
- Place spaghetti sauce in saucepan with 1 cup (240 ml) mozzarella cheese and heat slightly, but do not boil.
- Spoon about half sauce over spaghetti and arrange chicken breast over top. Spoon remaining spaghetti sauce on chicken and sprinkle remaining cheese over top.

■

Bread Sticks

1½ cups shredded Monterey Jack cheese   **360 ml**
¼ cup poppy seeds   **60 ml**
2 tablespoons dry onion soup mix   **30 ml**
2 (11 ounce) cans breadstick dough   **2 (312 g)**

- Spread cheese evenly in 9 x 13-inch (23 x 33 cm) baking dish. Sprinkle poppy seeds and soup mix evenly over cheese. Separate breadstick dough into sticks.
- Stretch strips slightly until each strip is about 12 inches (32 cm) long. Place strips one at a time into cheese mixture. Turn to coat all sides.
- Cut into 3 or 4-inch (8 cm) strips. Place on cookie sheet and bake at 375° (190° C) for about 12 minutes.

Home Sweet Home

EDITORS CHOICE

Easy Chicken and Dumplings

3 cups cooked, chopped chicken	710 ml
2 (10 ounce) cans cream of chicken soup	2 (280 g)
3 teaspoons chicken bouillon granules	15 ml
1 (8 ounce) can refrigerated buttermilk biscuits	227 g

- Combine chopped chicken, both cans of soup, chicken bouillon granules and 4½ cups (1.1 L) water in large kettle or Dutch oven. Boil mixture and stir to mix well.

- Separate biscuits and cut in half, cut again making 4 pieces out of each biscuit. Drop biscuit pieces, 1 at a time, into boiling chicken mixture and stir gently.

- When all biscuits are dropped, reduce heat to low and simmer, stirring occasionally, for about 15 minutes.

TIP: Deli turkey will work just fine in this recipe. It's a great time-saver!

■

Glazed Carrots

1 (16 ounce) package frozen baby carrots	.5 kg
¼ cup apple cider	60 ml
¼ cup apple jelly	60 ml
1½ teaspoons dijon-style mustard	7 ml

- Place carrots and apple cider in saucepan and bring to boil. Reduce heat, cover and simmer about 8 minutes until carrots are tender.

- Remove cover and cook on medium heat until liquid evaporates. Stir in jelly and mustard. Cook until jelly melts and carrots glaze.

Mom's Specialty

EDITORS CHOICE

Chicken Pot Pie

1 (15 ounce) package refrigerated piecrust	425 g
1 (19 ounce) can cream of chicken soup	538 g
2 cups diced chicken breast	480 ml
1 (10 ounce) package frozen mixed vegetables, thawed	280 ml

- Preheat oven to 325° (162° C). Line 1 layer piecrust in 9-inch (23 cm) pie plate. Fill with chicken soup, chicken and mixed vegetables.
- Cover with second layer of piecrust; fold edges under and crimp. With knife, cut 4 slits in center of piecrust. Bake uncovered for1 hour 15 minutes or until crust is golden.

TIP: *When you're too busy to cook a chicken, get the rotisserie chickens from the grocery store. They are great.*

■

Banana Split Pie

3 small bananas	Whipped topping
1 graham cracker piecrust	Chopped pecans
1 quart vanilla ice cream, softened	Maraschino cherries
Fudge sauce	

- Slice bananas and place on 6 ounce (168 g) graham cracker piecrust. Spoon softened ice cream over bananas. Freeze for 2 to 3 hours.
- Spread some fudge sauce over ice cream and top with layer of whipped topping and pecans. When ready to serve, place cherry on top of each piece of pie.

Serve It Up

Chicken-Broccoli Skillet

3 cups cooked, cubed chicken	710 ml
1 (16 ounce) package frozen broccoli florets	.5 kg
1 (8 ounce) package cubed processed cheese	227 g
⅔ cup mayonnaise	160 ml

- Combine chicken, broccoli, cheese and ¼ cup (60 ml) water in skillet. Cover and cook over medium heat until broccoli is crisp-tender and cheese melts. Stir in mayonnaise and heat through, but do not boil.

TIP: This is great served over hot cooked rice.

■

Marinated Corn Salad

3 (15 ounce) cans whole kernel corn, drained	3 (425 g)
1 red bell pepper, chopped	
1 cup chopped walnuts	240 ml
¾ cup chopped celery	180 ml
1 (8 ounce) bottle Italian salad dressing	227 g

- In bowl with lid, combine corn, bell pepper, walnuts and celery. (For a special little zip, add several dashes hot sauce.)
- Pour salad dressing over vegetables and refrigerate several hours before serving.

Feel Good Supper

Chicken and Noodles

1 (3 ounce) package chicken-flavored, instant ramen noodles	84 g
1 (16 ounce) package frozen broccoli, cauliflower and carrots	.5 kg
⅔ cup sweet-and-sour sauce	160 ml
3 boneless, skinless chicken breast halves, cooked	

- Cook noodles and vegetables in saucepan with 2 cups (480 ml) boiling water for 3 minutes, stir occasionally and drain.
- Combine noodle-vegetable mixture with seasoning packet, sweet-and-sour sauce and a little salt and pepper. Cut chicken in strips, add chicken to noodle mixture and heat thoroughly.

TIP: *You may want to add 1 tablespoon (15 ml) soy sauce, if you have it on hand.*

■

Creamy Cherry-Lime Pie

2 (8 ounce) cartons lime yogurt	2 (227 g)
⅓ cup chopped maraschino cherries, divided	80 ml
1 (8 ounce) carton frozen whipped topping, thawed	227 g
1 (6 ounce) graham cracker piecrust	168 g

- Stir together yogurt and ¼ cup (60 ml) cherries. Fold in whipped topping.
- Spoon mixture into graham cracker crust and garnish with chopped cherries. Refrigerate 6 to 8 hours or until firm.

■ ■ ■

Cheesy Chicken

Asparagus-Cheese Chicken

1 tablespoon butter	15 ml
4 boneless, skinless chicken breast halves	
1 (10 ounce) can broccoli-cheese soup	280 g
1 (10 ounce) package frozen asparagus cuts	280 g
⅓ cup milk	80 ml
1 (3.5 ounce) box boil-in-bag success rice	100 g

- Heat butter in skillet and cook chicken for 10 to 15 minutes or until brown on both sides. Remove chicken and set aside.
- In same skillet, combine soup, asparagus and milk. Bring to a boil, return chicken to skillet and reduce heat to low.
- Cover and cook another 25 minutes until chicken is no longer pink and asparagus is tender. Cook rice according to package directions and serve with chicken over rice.

■

Cheesy Vegetable Salad

2 seedless cucumbers, peeled, coarsely chopped	
1 sweet red bell pepper, julienned	
1 sweet onion, coarsely chopped	
1 cup crumbled feta cheese	240 ml

- In salad bowl, combine cucumbers, bell pepper, onion and feta cheese and toss with ? cups (160 ml) vinaigrette salad dressing.

TIP: *Check with your grocer to find out when he gets Vidalia onions from Georgia or 1015 Texas Super Sweets. They are great.*

Chicken Squares

2 (12 ounce) cans chicken breast chunks with liquid	2 (340 g)
1 (8 ounce) carton cream cheese, softened	227 g
¼ cup finely chopped onion	60 ml
2 tablespoons sesame seeds	30 ml
1 (8 count) package refrigerated crescent rolls	

- Preheat oven to 350° (176° C). Drain chicken and pour liquid in mixing bowl. Combine chicken liquid with cream cheese and beat until creamy. Add chicken, onion and sesame seeds.
- Open package of crescent rolls and keep 2 triangles together to form 4 squares. Pinch seam together in middle of each square.
- Spoon about ½ cup (120 ml) chicken mixture into center of each square. Fold corners up into center and seal edges. Repeat for all squares. Place rolls on sprayed baking sheet and bake about 15 minutes.

■

Corn Pudding

3 (11 ounce) cans mexicorn, drained, divided	3 (312 g)
⅔ cup milk	160 ml
¼ cup (½ stick) butter, melted	60 ml
3 tablespoons sugar	45 ml
3 tablespoons flour	45 ml
4 large eggs, beaten	
1 (4 ounce) can chopped pimento, drained	114 g

- Preheat oven to 350° (176° C). Process 2 cans corn, milk, butter, sugar, flour and eggs in food processor or blender until mixture blends well. Stir in remaining corn and pimento and place in sprayed 2-quart (2 L) baking dish.
- Bake, uncovered, for 55 minutes or until top is golden brown.

■ ■ ■

Touch of Green

Creamy Chicken-Pasta

1 (10 ounce) package penne pasta	280 g
1 tablespoon olive oil	15 ml
2 (12 ounce) cans white chicken meat, drained	2 (340 g)
2 tablespoons prepared pesto	30 ml
¾ cup whipping cream	180 ml

- In large saucepan, cook penne pasta according to package directions. Drain and place back in saucepan. Gently stir in oil, chicken, pesto and whipping cream.
- Place saucepan over low heat, simmer just until cream is absorbed. Spoon into serving bowl and serve immediately.

■

Asparagus With Citrus Dressing

2 bunches fresh asparagus, ends trimmed

- Boil about 2 cups (480 ml) water with ½ teaspoon (2 ml) salt in large skillet and bring to a boil. Add asparagus and cook until tender, about 8 minutes. Drain asparagus on cloth towel to cool.

Citrus Dressing:

3 tablespoons extra-virgin olive oil	45 ml
⅔ cup fresh orange juice	160 ml
1 teaspoon orange zest	5 ml

- Combine oil, orange juice, orange zest and ½ teaspoon (2 ml) pepper in small bowl and mix well. Spoon dressing over asparagus and serve immediately.

Tortellini and Deviled

Tortellini-Chicken Supper

1 (9 ounce) package refrigerated cheese tortellini	255 g
1 (10 ounce) package frozen green peas, thawed	280 g
1 (8 ounce) carton cream cheese with chives and onion	227 g
½ cup sour cream	120 ml
1 (9 ounce) package frozen, cooked chicken breasts	255 g

- Cook tortellini in saucepan according to package directions. Place peas in colander and pour hot pasta water over peas. Return tortellini and peas to saucepan.
- Combine cream cheese and sour cream in smaller saucepan, heat on low and stir well until cream cheese melts. Spoon mixture over tortellini and peas, toss and keep heat on low.
- Heat cooked chicken in microwave according to package directions. Spoon tortellini and peas in serving bowl and place chicken on top. Serve hot.

■

A Different Deviled Egg

10 large eggs, hard-boiled, peeled	
⅔ cup creamy dijon-style gourmayo	160 ml
2 tablespoons fresh snipped parsley	30 ml
1 teaspoon dried dill weed	5 ml
2 teaspoons dried chives	10 ml

- Cut off tops (about ⅓-inch/.8 cm) of each egg, scoop out yolks and place in mixing bowl. Carefully cut thin slice from bottom of egg so egg will sit level.
- Mash yolks with fork and add gourmayo, parsley, dill weed, chives and salt and pepper to taste. Carefully stuff each egg with yolk mixture and place on serving plate sitting up.

Chicken Over Rice

Glazed Chicken Over Rice

4 boneless, skinless chicken breast halves, cubed
1 (20 ounce) can pineapple chunks with juice   567 g
½ cup honey mustard grill-and-glaze sauce   120 ml
1 red bell pepper, seeded, chopped
2 cups instant white rice, cooked   480 ml

- Place a little oil in skillet and brown chicken. Reduce heat and cook 15 minutes. Add pineapple, honey mustard sauce and bell pepper and bring to a boil.
- Reduce heat and simmer for 15 minutes or until sauce thickens slightly. Serve over hot cooked rice.

■

Creamy Cauliflower

1 head cauliflower, broken into large florets
1 red bell pepper, chopped
1 small zucchini, chopped
1 (10 ounce) can cream of celery soup   280 ml
⅓ cup milk   80 ml

- Place cauliflower florets, red bell pepper and zucchini in saucepan with about ¾ cup (180 ml) water and a little salt. Cover and cook on high heat about 10 minutes or until cauliflower is tender. Drain.
- In smaller saucepan, heat soup and milk and stir until it mixes well. Spoon cauliflower, bell pepper and zucchini into serving bowl and pour soup mixture over vegetables. Serve immediately.

Sweet 'N Spicy

Sweet 'N Spicy Chicken

1 pound boneless, skinless chicken breast halves	.5 kg
1 (1 ounce) packet taco seasoning	28 g
1 (16 ounce) jar chunky salsa	.5 kg
1 (12 ounce) jar peach preserves	340 g
Hot cooked rice	

- Cut chicken into ½-inch (1.2 cm) cubes and place in large, plastic bag. Add taco seasoning and toss to coat.
- In skillet, brown chicken in a little oil. Combine salsa and preserves, stir into skillet and bring mixture to a boil.
- Reduce heat, cover and simmer until chicken juices run clear, about 15 minutes. Serve over hot cooked rice.

■

Parmesan Asparagus

1 bunch fresh asparagus	
1 tablespoon olive oil	15 ml
2 tablespoons lemon juice	30 ml
⅓ cup fresh grated parmesan cheese	80 ml

- Trim woody ends from asparagus and discard. Saute asparagus in oil in large skillet over medium heat just until tender-crisp and still bright green in color.
- Remove from heat and add lemon juice and salt and pepper to taste. Sprinkle with parmesan cheese and serve.

■ ■ ■

Chicken and Potatoes

EDITORS CHOICE

Cheesy Crusted Chicken

¾ cup mayonnaise (not light)	180 ml
½ cup grated parmesan cheese	120 ml
5 - 6 boneless, skinless chicken breast halves	
1 cup Italian seasoned dry breadcrumbs	240 ml

- Preheat oven to 400° (204° C). Combine mayonnaise and cheese. Place chicken breasts on wax paper and spread mayonnaise-cheese mixture over chicken. Sprinkle both sides heavily with dry breadcrumbs
- Place chicken in large sprayed baking pan with pieces not touching. Bake for 20 minutes (25 minutes if chicken pieces are fairly large). Slice chicken and place on serving platter.

■

Rosemary New Potatoes

2 pounds small new potatoes, halved	
¼ cup olive oil	60 ml
1 teaspoon dried rosemary	5 ml
1 teaspoon seasoned salt	5 ml

- Place potatoes in saucepan with about 1-inch (2.5 cm) water and a little salt. Cover and cook on medium heat, turning occasionally, until tender (about 15 minutes). Drain and toss with olive oil, rosemary, seasoned salt and plenty of black pepper. Cover again to keep warm.

■ ■ ■

Cacciatore Night

Chicken Cacciatore

1 (2 pound) frying chicken, quartered	1 kg
2 onions, sliced	
Hot cooked noodles	

Sauce:

1 (15 ounce) can stewed tomatoes	425 g
1 (8 ounce) can tomato sauce	227 g
1 teaspoon dried oregano	5 ml
1 teaspoon celery seed	5 ml

- Quarter chicken and sprinkle with plenty of salt and pepper. Place in large skillet on medium to high heat, with a little oil. Add sliced onions and cook until chicken is tender, about 15 minutes.

- Add stewed tomatoes, tomato sauce, oregano and celery seed. Bring mixture to a boil, reduce heat and simmer uncovered for about 20 minutes. Serve over hot cooked noodles or spaghetti.

■

Oven-Baked Asparagus

1 bunch fresh asparagus, trimmed	
2 tablespoons extra-virgin olive oil	30 ml
2 tablespoons balsamic vinegar	30 ml
⅓ cup fresh grated parmesan cheese	80 ml

- Preheat oven to 400° (204° C). Arrange asparagus in single layer in shallow baking dish and drizzle olive oil over asparagus. Bake uncovered about 10 minutes or until asparagus is tender.

- To serve, sprinkle with a little salt and pepper, balsamic vinegar and parmesan cheese.

■ ■ ■

Green Pea Stand-By

Creamy Broccoli Chicken

5 large boneless, skinless chicken breast halves
2 (10 ounce) cans creamy chicken verde soup   2 (280 g)
½ cup milk   120 ml
1 (16 ounce) package frozen broccoli florets, thawed .5 kg

- In very large skillet with lid sprinkle chicken with salt and pepper and brown breasts in a little oil.   On medium-high heat, stir both cans of soup and milk into skillet.
- Stir to mix and as you stir, spoon soup mixture over top of chicken breasts.   When mixture mixes well and is hot, reduce heat, cover and simmer for 20 minutes.
- Place broccoli florets around chicken and into creamy sauce. Return heat to high until broccoli is hot.   Reduce heat and simmer about 10 minutes or until broccoli is tender-crisp.

TIP: *This is great over Uncle Ben's 8.8 ounce/255 g package ready rice. Just microwave it and in 90 seconds it's done*

■

Colorful English Pea Salad

2 (16 ounce) packages frozen green peas,
**   thawed, drained   2 (.5 kg)**
1 (12 ounce) package cubed mozzarella cheese   340 g
1 red and 1 orange bell pepper, chopped
1 onion, chopped
1¼ cups mayonnaise   300 ml

- In large salad bowl, combine uncooked peas, cubed cheese, bell peppers and onion and toss to mix.   Stir in mayonnaise and salt and pepper to taste.   Chill before serving.

Honey All Around

Honey-Glazed Chicken

4 boneless, skinless chicken breast halves	
½ cup refrigerated dijon-style honey-mustard salad dressing	120 ml
1 green and 1 red bell pepper, julienned	
1 (20 ounce) can pineapple chunks with juice	567 g
1 (10 ounce) box original couscous	280 g

- Cut chicken breasts into strips, add a little salt and pepper and brown in large skillet with a little oil. Add juice from pineapple, cover and simmer for 15 minutes.

- Add honey-mustard dressing, julienned peppers and pineapple chunks to chicken, bring to a boil, reduce heat, cover and simmer for another 15 minutes.

- Cook couscous according to package directions and serve chicken casserole over hot, cooked couscous.

■

Seasoned Zucchini and Leeks

¼ cup (½ stick) butter	60 ml
2 large leeks, finely chopped	
6 medium zucchini, chopped	
1 teaspoon garlic powder	5 ml
1 teaspoon seasoned salt	5 ml

- Place butter in skillet and saute leeks about 2 minutes. Stir in zucchini, garlic and seasoned salt.

- Cover and cook on medium heat for 15 minutes, stirring occasionally or until most liquid evaporates. Serve immediately.

Potato and Spinach

The Perfect Potato

4 large baking potatoes, baked	
4 tablespoons (½ stick) butter	60 ml
¼ cup sour cream	60 ml
1 cup finely chopped deli turkey	240 ml
1 (10 ounce) package frozen broccoli florets, chopped, cooked	280 g
1 cup shredded sharp cheddar cheese	240 ml

- Preheat oven to 400° (204° C). Cut potatoes down center, but not through to bottom. For each potato, use 1 tablespoon (15 ml) butter and 1 tablespoon (15 ml) sour cream. With fork, work in ¼ cup (60 ml) turkey, one-fourth of broccoli and ¼ cup (60 ml) cheese.
- Just before serving, place potatoes on baking sheet and heat for 10 minutes.

■

Spinach and Apple Salad

1 (10 ounce) package fresh spinach	280 g
⅓ cup frozen orange juice concentrate, thawed	80 ml
¼ cup mayonnaise	60 ml
1 red apple with peel, diced	
5 slices bacon, fried, crumbled	

- Tear spinach into small pieces.
- Mix orange juice concentrate and mayonnaise.
- When ready to serve, mix spinach and apple (cut apple at the last minute), pour dressing over salad and top with bacon.

Honey Skillet

Lemon-Honey Glazed Chicken

1 (2½ pound) chicken, quartered	1.2 kg
⅓ cup honey	80 ml
2 tablespoons lemon juice	30 ml
1 tablespoon dry onion soup mix	15ml

- Preheat oven to 375° (190° C). Place chicken quarters, skin side down on sprayed 9 x 13-inch (23 x 33 cm) baking pan. Bake uncovered for 30 minutes. Remove from oven and turn chicken quarters over.

- Combine honey, lemon juice and onion soup mix in small bowl and brush glaze over chicken. Continue cooking, uncovered, another 20 minutes and brush glaze over chicken every 5 minutes.

■

Skillet Ravioli and Broccoli

1 (16 ounce) package refrigerated cheese ravioli	.5 kg
1 (16 ounce) package frozen broccoli, thawed	.5 kg
1 (16 ounce) carton marinara sauce	.5 kg
¾ cup shredded mozzarella cheese	180 ml

- In large saucepan with boiling water, cook ravioli 8 minutes or until tender. Drain ravioli and return to saucepan.

- Cook broccoli according to package directions and drain. Stirring ravioli gently, add broccoli and marinara sauce to saucepan. Cook on medium heat, stirring often, just until mixture is thoroughly hot. Sprinkle with cheese, cover and cook 1 minute until cheese melts.

Parmesan and Alfredo

Parmesan Chicken

1 (1 ounce) packet dry Italian salad dressing mix	28 g
½ cup grated parmesan cheese	120 ml
¼ cup flour	60 ml
¾ teaspoon garlic powder	4 ml
5 boneless, skinless chicken breast halves	

- Preheat oven to 375° (190° C). In shallow bowl, combine salad dressing mix, cheese, flour and garlic. Moisten chicken with a little water and coat with cheese mixture. Place in sprayed 9 x 13-inch (23 x 33 cm) baking pan.
- Bake for 25 minutes or until chicken is light brown and thoroughly cooked.

■

Wonderful Alfredo Fettuccine

1 (16 ounce) package uncooked fettuccine	.5 kg
2 tablespoons butter	30 ml
¾ cup grated fresh parmesan cheese	180 ml
1¼ cups whipping cream	300 ml

- Cook fettuccine according to package directions.
- In large saucepan over medium heat, melt butter and stir in parmesan cheese, whipping cream and black pepper to taste.
- Cook 1 minute and stir constantly. Reduce heat, pour in fettuccine and toss gently to coat fettuccine.

■ ■ ■

Family Choice

Skillet-Roasted Chicken

1 (2½ pound) chicken, quartered	1.2 kg
2 teaspoons sage	10 ml
2 teaspoons prepared minced garlic	10 ml
2 (10 ounce) cans cream of chicken soup	2 (280 g)
1 (8.8 ounce) package ready-roasted chicken rice	255 g

- Dry chicken quarters with paper towels and sprinkle with sage and salt and pepper to taste. Place in large skillet with a little oil. Cook on both sides over medium heat for 15 minutes.

- In saucepan, combine garlic, chicken soup and ½ cup (120 ml) water; heat just enough to blend ingredients. Pour over chicken, cover and cook on low heat for another 15 minutes.

- Cook rice in microwave according to package directions. Serve chicken over cooked rice.

■

Cheesy Macaroni-Stuffed Peppers

4 large green bell peppers	
1 (22 ounce) carton refrigerated macaroni and cheese	624 g
1 cup shredded cheddar cheese	240 ml

- Preheat oven to 350° (176° C). Cut peppers in half lengthwise and remove seeds and veins. Steam, covered in simmering water, for 8 minutes; drain well.

- Heat macaroni and cheese in microwave according to package directions and fill each pepper half with macaroni and cheese. Place in sprayed baking dish. Bake 10 minutes.

- Remove from oven, sprinkle 1 heaping tablespoon cheddar cheese over each pepper and return to oven for 5 minutes.

■ ■ ■

Honey Roaster

Honey-Roasted Chicken

3 tablespoons soy sauce	45 ml
3 tablespoon honey	45 ml
2½ cups crushed wheat cereal	600 ml
½ cup very finely minced walnuts	120 ml
5 - 6 boneless, skinless chicken breast halves	

- Preheat oven to 400° (104° C). In shallow bowl, combine soy sauce and honey and set aside. In another shallow bowl, combine crushed cereal and walnuts.
- Dip both sides of each chicken breasts in soy sauce-honey mixture and dredge in cereal-walnut mixture. Place each piece on sprayed foil-lined baking sheet. Bake for 25 minutes (about 35 minutes if breasts are very large).

■

Skillet Beans and Rice

6 slices bacon, cut in 1-inch pieces	2.5 cm
1 (15 ounce) can Mexican-stewed tomatoes	425 g
1 cup uncooked instant rice	240 ml
2 (15 ounce) cans chili beans with juice	2 (425 g)

- In skillet fry bacon until crisp, drain but save 2 tablespoons (30 ml) drippings. Set bacon pieces aside.
- Dry skillet with paper towels and stir in stewed tomatoes, rice, bacon drippings and 1 cup (240 ml) water. Bring to a boil, reduce heat and simmer 3 minutes or until rice is tender and most of liquid evaporates.
- Add chili beans and cook until mixture is thoroughly hot. Serve right from skillet or spoon into serving bowl and top with bacon pieces.

Made In The Shade

Summertime Limeade Chicken

6 large boneless, skinless chicken breast halves	
1 (6 ounce) can frozen limeade concentrate, thawed	168 g
3 tablespoons brown sugar	45 ml
½ cup chili sauce	120 ml
2 (6 ounce) package garlic and butter-flavored rice	2 (168 g)

- Sprinkle chicken breasts with salt and pepper and place in sprayed skillet over high heat. Cook and brown on both sides for about 10 minutes. Remove from skillet and set aside keeping warm.

- Add limeade concentrate, brown sugar and chili sauce to skillet and bring to a boil. Cook, stirring constantly for 4 minutes. Return chicken to skillet and spoon sauce over chicken.

- Reduce heat, cover and simmer for 15 minutes. Cook rice according to package directions and serve chicken over cooked rice.

■

Caramelized Carrots

1 (16 ounce) package baby carrots	.5 kg
2 teaspoons soy sauce	10 ml
2 tablespoons brown sugar	30 ml
1 tablespoon olive oil	15 ml

- Preheat oven to 425° (220° C). Place carrots in single layer in sprayed 7 x 11-inch (18 x 28 cm) baking pan. Combine soy sauce, brown sugar, olive oil and a little salt. Spoon over carrots.

- Bake for 15 minutes and stir once.

■ ■ ■

Cruisin'

Sweet-Spicy Chicken Thighs

3 tablespoons chili powder	45 ml
3 tablespoons honey	45 ml
2 tablespoons lemon juice	30 ml
10 - 12 boneless, skinless chicken thighs	

- Preheat oven to 425° (220° C). Line 10 x 15-inch (25 x 38 cm) shallow baking pan with heavy foil. Combine chili powder, honey, lemon juice and salt and pepper to taste.
- Brush mixture over chicken thighs and turn thighs to coat completely. Bake, turning over once, for about 35 minutes.

■

Cheesy New Potatoes

½ cup (1 stick) butter, melted	120 ml
¼ cup grated parmesan cheese	60 ml
12 medium new potatoes	

- Preheat oven to 325° (162° C). Melt butter in 9 x 13-inch (23 x 33 cm) baking dish and sprinkle cheese and a little salt and pepper over butter.
- Cut potatoes in half, place cut side down in baking dish and spoon butter-cheese mixture over potatoes every 15 minutes. Bake uncovered for 30 minutes or until potatoes are tender.

■ ■ ■

In The Skillet

Tasty Skillet Chicken

5 large boneless, skinless chicken breast halves
1 green and 1 red bell pepper, julienned
2 small yellow squash, seeded, julienned
1 (16 ounce) bottle thick-and-chunky salsa .5 kg

- Cut chicken breasts into thin strips. With a little oil in large skillet, saute chicken for about 5 minutes. Add peppers and squash and cook another 5 minutes or until peppers are tender-crisp.

- Stir in salsa and bring to a boil, lower heat and simmer for 10 minutes. Serve over hot buttered rice.

TIP: *The easiest way to serve hot buttered rice is to buy 1 (8.8 ounce/ 255 g) package ready buttery rice. You can microwave it in 90 seconds. You will need 2 packages for the chicken in this recipe.*

■

Brown Sugar Carrots

¼ cup (½ stick) butter 60 ml
¾ cup packed brown sugar 180 ml
½ teaspoon cinnamon 2 ml
2 (16 ounce) packages peeled baby carrots 2 (.5 kg)

- In skillet, combine butter, brown sugar, cinnamon and ½ cup (120 ml) water; cook on medium heat until bubbly. Stir in carrots, cover and cook on medium heat until carrots are glazed and tender.

Light and Fruity

Strawberry-Chicken Salad

1 pound boneless, skinless chicken breast halves	.5 kg
1 (10 ounce) package spring greens mix	280 g
1 pint fresh strawberries, sliced	.5 kg
½ cup chopped walnuts	120 ml
¾ cup honey	180 ml
⅔ cup red wine vinegar	160 ml
1 tablespoon soy sauce	15 ml
½ teaspoon ground ginger	2 ml

- Cut chicken into strips and place in large skillet with a little oil. Cook and stir on medium-high heat for about 10 minutes.
- While chicken is cooking, combine honey, vinegar, soy sauce and ginger; mix well. After chicken strips cook 10 minutes, pour ½ cup (120 ml) dressing into skillet with chicken and cook 2 minutes longer or until liquid evaporates. In salad bowl, combine greens mix, strawberries, walnuts and remaining dressing; toss. Top with chicken strips.

■

Lariat Bread Knots

¼ cup (½ stick) butter	60 ml
½ teaspoon chili powder	2 ml
½ teaspoon ground cumin	2 ml
1 (11 ounce) can refrigerated breadsticks	312 g

- Preheat oven to 350° (176° C). In saucepan, melt butter and stir in chili powder and ground cumin. Unroll breadsticks and separate each portion.
- Loosely tie each portion into a knot and place on sprayed baking sheet about 1-inch (2.5 cm) apart. With kitchen brush, spread butter mixture evenly over bread knots and bake 15 minutes or until breadsticks are light brown.

Crunchy Chicken

Chicken Crunch

4 boneless, skinless chicken breast halves
½ cup Italian salad dressing   120 ml
½ cup sour cream   120 ml
2½ cups cornflakes, crushed   600 ml

- Place chicken in sealed plastic bag; add salad dressing and sour cream. Seal, refrigerate 1 hour. Remove chicken from marinade, discarding marinade.
- Dredge chicken in cornflakes; place in sprayed 9 x 13-inch (23 x 33 cm) baking dish.
- Bake at 375° (190° C) for 45 minutes.

■

Cauliflower-Bacon Salad

1 large head cauliflower, cut into florets
1 red and 1 green bell pepper, chopped
1½ cups cubed mozzarella cheese   360 ml
1 (6 ounce) package cooked, crumbled bacon   168 g
1 bunch fresh green onions, sliced

- In plastic bowl with lid, combine all salad ingredients.

Dressing:

1 cup mayonnaise   240 ml
1 tablespoon sugar   15 ml
1 tablespoon lemon juice   15 ml

- In small bowl, combine mayonnaise, sugar, lemon juice, 1 teaspoon (5 ml) salt plus a little pepper and stir to blend well. Spoon dressing over salad and toss to coat. Cover and refrigerate several hours before serving.

■ ■ ■

All-Time Favorites

Chicken-Green Bean Bake

2 cups instant rice	480 ml
1 (16 ounce) package shredded processed cheese	.5 kg
1 (16 ounce) package frozen cut green beans, thawed	.5 kg
3 cups cooked, cubed chicken	710 ml
2 cups coarsely crushed potato chips	480 ml

- Preheat oven to 325° (162° C). Cook rice in large saucepan according to package directions and stir in cheese and extra ¼ cup (60 ml) water. Stir and mix until cheese melts.
- Cook green beans according to package directions; drain. Stir in rice mixture; add cubed chicken and mix well. Spoon into sprayed 9 x 13-inch (23 x 33 cm) baking dish. Top with crushed potato chips and bake 20 minutes or until chips are light brown.

■

Holiday-Cranberry Salad

1 (20 ounce) can crushed pineapple with juice	567 g
1 (6 ounce) package raspberry flavor gelatin	168 g
1 red delicious apple, chopped	
¾ cup chopped pecans	180 ml
1 (16 ounce) can whole berry cranberry sauce	.5 kg

- Drain pineapple juice into measuring cup and add water to equal 1½ cups (360 ml) liquid. Pour into saucepan and bring to a boil. Remove from heat and stir in gelatin until it dissolves.
- Add pineapple, apple, pecans and cranberry sauce and stir until it mixes well. Pour into 7 x 11-inch (18 x 28 cm) glass dish and refrigerate overnight or at least 4 hours.
- Cut into squares and place on individual salad plates over shredded lettuce.

■ ■ ■

Diner's Choice

Turkey and Rice Olé

This may be served as a main course or as a sandwich wrap in flour tortillas.

1 pound ground turkey	.5 kg
1 (5.5 ounce) package Mexican rice mix	155 g
2 (15 ounce) cans black beans, rinsed, drained	2 (425 g)
1½ cups thick-and-chunky salsa	360 ml

- In large skillet, brown turkey and break up chunks with fork. Add rice mix and 2 cups (480 ml) water, bring to a boil and reduce heat. Simmer about 8 minutes or until rice is tender. Stir in beans and salsa and cook just until mixture is completely hot.

■

Broccoli Fritters

1 (16 ounce) package frozen chopped broccoli	.5 kg
2 eggs, lightly beaten	
1 small onion, chopped	
½ cup chopped pecans	120 ml
½ cup self-rising flour	120 ml

- Cook broccoli according to package directions and drain well. Combine broccoli, eggs, onion, pecans and flour and mix well.
- Place about ¼-inch (.6 cm) oil in skillet and heat. Drop broccoli mixture by tablespoonfuls into hot oil and cook in batches for 2 minutes on each side or until lightly brown.
- Remove to wire rack on baking pan and keep warm at 200° (93° C) in oven until each batch cooks.

Tender Goodness

Turkey Tenders with Honey-Ginger Glaze

1 pound turkey tenders	.5 kg
Oil	
1 (6 ounce) roasted-garlic long grain, wild rice	168 g
⅔ cup honey	160 ml
2 teaspoons grated, peeled fresh ginger	10 ml
1 tablespoon soy sauce	15 ml
1 tablespoon lemon juice	15 ml

- Place a little oil in heavy skillet and cook turkey tenders about 5 minutes on each side or until brown.
- Combine all honey, ginger, soy sauce and lemon juice, mix well and pour into skillet. Bring mixture to a boil, reduce heat and simmer for 15 minutes. Serve turkey tenders over hot cooked rice.

■

Baked Asparagus with Lemon Dressing

2 bunches fresh asparagus	
2 tablespoons olive oil	30 ml
¼ cup lemon juice	60 ml
2 tablespoons finely minced green onions	30 ml
S! cup olive oil	80 ml
2 eggs, hard-boiled, finely minced	

- Preheat oven to 375° (190° C). Place asparagus on rimmed baking sheet, drizzle with olive oil and sprinkle with 1 teaspoon (5 ml) salt. Toss to spread oil evenly and bake for 15 minutes.
- Mix lemon juice, green onions, a little salt and slowly whisk in oil to blend well. Arrange asparagus on serving platter and drizzle with lemon juice-olive oil mixture. Garnish with minced eggs.

■ ■ ■

Day-After-Thanksgiving

Turkey-Broccoli Bake

1 (16 ounce) package frozen broccoli spears, thawed	.5 kg
2 cups cooked, diced turkey	480 ml

Sauce:

1 (10 ounce) can cream of chicken soup	280 g
½ cup mayonnaise	120 ml
2 tablespoons lemon juice	30 ml
⅓ cup grated parmesan cheese	80 ml

- Preheat oven to 350° (176° C). Arrange broccoli spears in bottom of sprayed 9 x 13-inch (23 x 33 cm) baking dish and sprinkle with diced turkey.

- In saucepan, combine chicken soup, mayonnaise, lemon juice, cheese and ¼ cup (60 ml) water. Heat just enough to mix well. Spoon over broccoli and turkey. Cover and bake for 20 minutes, uncover and continue baking for another 15 minutes.

■

Jack's Breadsticks

1 (11 ounce) can refrigerated breadstick dough	312 g
⅓ cup finely shredded Monterey Jack cheese with jalapenos	80 ml
½ teaspoon ground cumin	2 ml
½ teaspoon garlic powder	2 ml

- Preheat oven to 375° (190° C). Place dough on flat surface and cut along perforations to form 12 breadsticks. Combine cheese, cumin and garlic powder, sprinkle over breadsticks and press into dough.

- Twist each breadstick and place on sprayed baking sheet. Bake for 14 minutes or until light brown.

■ ■ ■

Turkey Surprise

Turkey and Rice Supper

¾ pound cooked, sliced turkey	340 g
2 cups cooked instant brown rice	480 ml
1 (10 ounce) can cream of chicken soup	280 g
1 (10 ounce) can chopped tomatoes and green chilies	280 g
1½ cups crushed tortilla chips	360 ml

- Preheat oven to 350° (176° C). Place turkey slices in bottom of sprayed 7 x 11-inch (18 x 28 cm) baking dish.
- In bowl, combine rice, chicken soup and tomatoes and mix well. Spoon over turkey slices. Sprinkle crushed tortilla chips over top of casserole and bake, uncovered, for 40 minutes.

■

Coleslaw with Buttermilk Dressing

2 (10 ounce) packages finely shredded cabbage	2 (280 g)
1 carrot, shredded	
½ cup mayonnaise	120 ml
½ cup sugar	120 ml
½ cup buttermilk*	120 ml
3 tablespoons lemon juice	45 ml

- Place cabbage and carrot in salad bowl.
- Combine mayonnaise, sugar, buttermilk, lemon juice and 1 teaspoon (5 ml) salt in small bowl. Pour over cabbage and carrot and toss. Cover and chill at least 2 hours.

TIP: *To make buttermilk, mix 1 cup (240 ml) milk with 1 tablespoon (15 ml) lemon juice or vinegar and let milk rest about 10 minutes.*

Great Combination

Chilly Night's Turkey Bake

1 (6 ounce) package stuffing mix for chicken, divided	168 g
1½ pounds turkey, cut into 1-inch strips	360 ml/2.5 cm
1 (10 ounce) can cream of chicken soup	280 g
½ cup sour cream	120 ml
1 (16 ounce) package frozen mixed vegetables, thawed, drained	.5 kg

- Preheat oven to 375° (190° C). Sprinkle ½ cup (120 ml) dry stuffing mix evenly over bottom of sprayed 9 x 13-inch (23 x 33 cm) baking dish and set aside. In bowl, combine remaining stuffing and 1 cup (240 ml) water and stir just until moist and set aside.
- Place turkey strips over dry stuffing mix in baking dish. In bowl, mix soup, sour cream and vegetables, spoon over turkey strips and top with prepared stuffing. Bake, uncovered, for 25 minutes.

■

Berry Delicious Salad

1 (10 ounce) package mixed salad greens	280 g
2 cups fresh blueberries	480 ml
⅔ cup crumbled gorgonzola cheese	160 ml
⅓ cup chopped pecans, toasted	80 ml

- In salad bowl, combine salad greens, blueberries, cheese and pecans. Toss salad with raspberry vinaigrette and chill.

Pizza Lite

Pizza Pies

½ pound bulk turkey sausage	227 g
⅔ cup prepared pizza sauce	160 ml
1 (10 ounce) package refrigerated pizza dough	280 g
½ cup shredded mozzarella cheese	120 ml

- Preheat oven to 400° (204° C). In skillet, brown sausage and stir to break up pieces of meat. Drain sausage; add pizza sauce and heat until it bubbles.
- Unroll pizza dough, place on flat surface and pat into 8 x 12-inch (20 x 32 cm) rectangle. Cut into 6 squares. Divide sausage mixture evenly among squares and sprinkle with cheese.
- Lift 1 corner of each square and fold over filling to make triangle. Press edges together with fork to seal. Bake about 12 minutes or until light golden brown. Serve immediately.

■

Nutty Slaw

1 (16 ounce) package shredded carrots	.5 kg
3 cups shredded cabbage	710 ml
2 red delicious apples, diced	
¾ cup raisins	180 ml
¾ cup chopped walnuts	180 ml
1 (8 ounce) bottle coleslaw dressing	227 g

- In plastic bowl with lid, combine shredded carrots, shredded cabbage, apples, raisins and walnuts.
- Pour about three-fourths bottle of dressing over mixture and increase dressing as needed. Cover and refrigerate several hours before serving.

Italian Tonight

Ravioli and Tomatoes

1 (9 ounce) package sausage-filled ravioli	255 g
1 (15 ounce) can Italian-stewed tomatoes	425 g
2 (4 ounce) cans sliced mushrooms	2 (114 g)
1 (5 ounce) package grated parmesan cheese	143 g

- Cook ravioli according to package directions and drain well. Stir in stewed tomatoes and mushrooms and bring to a boil. Reduce heat to low and simmer for about 5 minutes.
- Transfer to serving dish and sprinkle cheese on each serving.

■

Red, White and Green Salad

3 small zucchini, thinly sliced	
2 red delicious apples with peel, chopped	
2 cups fresh broccoli florets	480 ml
¾ cup coarsely chopped walnuts	180 ml
1 (8 ounce) bottle creamy Italian salad dressing	227 g

- In salad bowl, combine zucchini, apples, broccoli and walnuts and toss.
- Pour about three-fourths bottle of salad dressing over salad and toss. Use more dressing if needed. Serve immediately.

■ ■ ■

This Will Work

Sausage Casserole

1 pound pork sausage	.5 kg
2 (15 ounce) cans pork and beans	2 (425 g)
1 (15 ounce) can Mexican-style stewed tomatoes	425 g
1 (8 ounce) package corn muffin mix	227 g

- Brown sausage and drain fat. Add beans and tomatoes, blend and bring to a boil.
- Pour into 3-quart (3 L) greased casserole. Prepare muffin mix according to package directions. Drop by teaspoonfuls over meat-bean mixture.
- Bake at 400° (204° C) for 30 minutes or until top is brown.

■

Caramel-Cinnamon Dessert

1 (5 ounce) package French vanilla instant pudding	143 g
3 cups milk	710 ml
1 (8 ounce) carton whipped topping	227 g
1 box cinnamon graham crackers	

- Combine pudding and milk and mix well. Fold in whipped topping. Line bottom of 9 x 13-inch (23 x 33 cm) glass dish with whole graham crackers.
- Put half pudding mixture over crackers and top with second layer of crackers. Spread remaining pudding over top. Top with remaining crackers. (There should be 2 or 3 left.)
- Add prepared caramel icing over last layer of graham crackers and refrigerate. (This is best when you make it a day in advance so pudding can soak into crackers.)

Colorful Bacon Dish

Bacon-Rice Dish

¾ pound bacon	180 ml
2½ cups cooked rice	600 ml
1 (15 ounce) can sliced carrots, drained	425 g
1 (10 ounce) package frozen green peas, thawed	280 g

- In large skillet, fry bacon until crisp and remove. Drain skillet partially, leaving about ½ cup (120 ml) bacon drippings in skillet. Crumble bacon and set aside.
- Add rice, carrots and peas to skillet and cook, stirring occasionally, until mixture heats thoroughly. Stir in bacon and serve hot.

■

Divinity Salad

1 (6 ounce) package lemon gelatin	168 g
1 (8 ounce) package cream cheese	227 g
¾ cup chopped pecans	180 ml
1 (15 ounce) can crushed pineapple with juice	425 g
1 (8 ounce) carton whipped topping	227 g

- With mixer, mix gelatin with 1 cup (240 ml) boiling water until well dissolved.
- Add cream cheese, beat slowly to start with, beat until smooth. Add pecans and pineapple. Cool in refrigerator until nearly set.
- Fold in whipped topping. Pour into 9 x 13-inch (23 x 33 cm) dish. Refrigerate.

■ ■ ■

Great Meal

Fruit-Covered Ham Slice

2 (15 ounce) cans fruit cocktail with juice	2 (425 g)
½ cup packed brown sugar	120 ml
2 tablespoons cornstarch	30 ml
1 (½-inch) thick center-cut ham slice	1.2 cm

- In saucepan, combine fruit cocktail, brown sugar and cornstarch; mix well. Cook and stir on medium heat, until sauce thickens.
- Place ham slice in large non-stick skillet on medium heat. Cook about 5 minutes or just until ham heats thoroughly. Place on serving platter and spoon fruit sauce over ham.

Spinach-Artichoke Bake

1 refrigerated pie crust (half of 15 ounce piecrust dough)	425 g
1 (8 ounce) package cream cheese, softened	227 g
1 (14 ounce) jar artichoke hearts, drained, chopped	396 g
1 (10 ounce) package frozen chopped spinach, thawed, drained	280 g
1 (1.8 ounce) box dry vegetable soup mix	57 g
1 (8 ounce) package shredded mozzarella cheese	227 g

- Preheat oven to 375° (190° C). Fit dough into 9-inch (23 cm) tart pan with removable sides. Pierce dough with fork several times.
- In mixing bowl, beat cream cheese until creamy and at low speed add artichokes, spinach, soup mix and half cheese. Spread evenly on crust. Sprinkle remaining cheese over top and bake 30 minutes or until light brown. Cool 15 minutes before serving and remove sides of pan.

Ham It Up

Tortellini and Ham Supper

2 (9 ounce) packages fresh tortellini	2 (255 g)
1 (10 ounce) package frozen green peas, thawed	280 g
1 (16 ounce) jar alfredo sauce	.5 kg
3 cups cubed ham	710 ml

- Cook tortellini according to package directions. Add green peas about 5 minutes before tortellini is done. Drain.
- In saucepan, heat alfredo sauce and ham until thoroughly hot. Toss with tortellini and peas. Serve immediately with hot French bread.

TIP: *This is a great recipe for leftover ham.*

■

Chilled Cranberry Salad

1 (14 ounce) can sweetened condensed milk	396 g
⅓ cup lemon juice	80 ml
1 (20 ounce) can crushed pineapple, drained	567 g
1 (16 ounce) can whole cranberry sauce	.5 kg
3 cups miniature marshmallows	710 ml
1 (8 ounce) carton whipped topping	227 g
Dash of red food coloring, optional	

- In large bowl, combine sweetened condensed milk and lemon juice and mix well. Add pineapple, cranberry sauce and marshmallows and stir until they blend well. Add food coloring for a brighter color.
- Fold in whipped topping and spoon into 9 x 13-inch (23 x 33 cm) dish. Let dish thaw for about 15 minutes before cutting into squares.

Best Ham

Cherry Best Ham

1 (½-inch) center-cut ham slice	1.2 cm
⅔ cup cherry preserves	160 ml
½ teaspoon ground cinnamon	2 ml
⅓ cup chopped walnuts	80 ml

- Preheat oven to 325° (162° C). Place ham slice on foil-lined 9 x 13-inch (23 x 33 cm) glass baking dish. Spread preserves over ham and sprinkle cinnamon on top. Sprinkle chopped walnuts over dish.
- Bake uncovered for 20 minutes. Serve right from baking dish.

■

Creamed Onions and Peas

1 (10 ounce) can cream of celery soup	280 g
½ cup milk	120 ml
3 (15 ounce) jars tiny white onions, drained	3 (425 g)
1 (10 ounce) package frozen peas	280 g
½ cup slivered almonds	120 ml
3 tablespoons grated parmesan cheese	45 ml

- Preheat oven to 350° (176° C). In large saucepan, combine soup and milk, heat and stir until bubbly. Gently stir in onions, peas and almonds and mix well. Spoon into sprayed 2-quart (2 L) baking dish. Sprinkle with parmesan cheese. Cover and bake for 30 minutes.

TIP: *For a colorful garnish, sprinkle a little paprika over top of casserole.*

■ ■ ■

Choice Ham

Sweet Potato Ham

1 (16 ounce/1½-inch) fully cooked ham slice	.5 kg/3 cm
1 (18 ounce) can sweet potatoes, drained	510 g
½ cup packed brown sugar	120 ml
⅓ cup chopped pecans	80 ml

- Slit outer edge of fat on ham slice at 1-inch (2.5 cm) intervals to prevent curling, but do not cut into ham. Place on 10-inch (25 cm) ovenproof, glass pie plate and broil for 5 minutes.
- In bowl, mash sweet potatoes with fork just once (not totally mashed). Add brown sugar and chopped pecans and mix well.
- Spoon mixture over ham slice and bake at 350° (176° C) for about 15 minutes. Serve right from pie plate.

■

Chilled Spinach Couscous

1 (10 ounce) package parmesan couscous	280 g
⅓ cup olive oil	80 ml
3 tablespoons lemon juice	45 ml
½ teaspoon sugar	2 ml
1 (9 ounce) package fresh baby spinach	255 g
4 fresh green onions, sliced	
2 tablespoons fresh chopped dill	30 ml
⅓ cup crumbled feta cheese	80 ml

- In large saucepan, cook couscous according to package directions. Fluff with fork and toss with olive oil, lemon juice and sugar; let cool completely.
- Tear stems from spinach. Stir onions, dill and spinach into chilled couscous; toss, cover and chill 2 hours.
- To serve, sprinkle feta cheese over top of salad.

■ ■ ■

Mix It Up

Ham and Veggies

2 (15 ounce) packages mixed vegetables	2 (425 g)
1 (10 ounce) can cream of celery soup	280 g
2 cups cubed, cooked ham	480 ml
½ teaspoon dried basil	2 ml

- Cook vegetables according to package directions. Add soup, ham and basil.
- Cook until mixture heats well and serve hot.

■

Carnival Cake

1 (18 ounce) white cake mix	510 g
2 (10 ounce) frozen sweetened strawberries with juice	2 (280 g)
1 (3 ounce) package instant vanilla pudding	84 g
1 (8 ounce) carton whipped topping	227 g

- Make cake mix according to package directions. Pour into greased 9 x 13-inch (23 x 33 cm) baking dish. Bake according to package directions.
- When cool, poke holes with knife in top of cake and pour strawberries over top. Prepare instant pudding with 1¼ cups (300 ml) milk.
- When it sets, pour over strawberries. Cover cake with whipped topping and refrigerate.

Honey, Dinner's Ready

Honey-Ham Slice

⅓ cup orange juice	80 ml
⅓ cup honey	80 ml
1 teaspoon prepared mustard	5 ml
1 (1-inch) thick slice fully cooked ham	2.5 cm

- Combine orange juice, honey and mustard in saucepan and cook slowly for 10 minutes, stirring occasionally.
- Place ham in broiling pan about 3 inches (8 cm) from heat. Brush with orange glaze.
- Broil for 8 minutes on first side. Turn ham slice over. Brush with glaze again and broil for another 6 to 8 minutes.

■

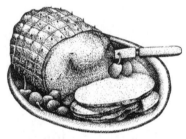

Cheddar-Broccoli Bake

1 (10 ounce) can cheddar cheese soup	280 g
½ cup milk	120 ml
1 (16 ounce) bag frozen broccoli florets, cooked	.5 kg
1 (3 ounce) can french-fried onion rings	84 g

- In 2-quart (2 L) baking dish, mix soup, milk and broccoli. Bake at 350° (176° C) for 25 minutes.
- Stir and sprinkle onions over broccoli mixture. Bake for 5 more minutes or until onions are golden.

Hammin' It Up

Supper In A Dish

2 (9 ounce) packages rice-in-a-bag	2 (255 g)
1½ cups cubed, cooked ham	360 ml
1½ cups shredded cheddar cheese	360 ml
1 (8 ounce) can green peas	227 g

- Prepare rice according to package directions. In large bowl, combine rice, ham, cheese and peas.
- Pour into 3-quart (3 L) baking dish and bake at 350° (176° C) for 15 to 20 minutes.

■

Five-Citrus Cream Pie

1 (14 ounce) can sweetened condensed milk	396 g
1 (6 ounce) can frozen five-citrus concentrate, partially thawed	168 g
1 (8 ounce) carton frozen whipped topping, thawed	227 g
1 (6 ounce) graham cracker piecrust	168 g

- Stir together sweetened condensed milk and five-citrus concentrate until they blend well. Fold in whipped topping.
- Spoon mixture into graham cracker crust. Refrigerate 6 to 8 hours.

■ ■ ■

Pork 'N Potatoes

Pork Chop Supper

1 (18 ounce) package smoked pork chops	510 g
1 (12 ounce) jar pork gravy	240 g
¼ cup milk	60 ml
1 (12 ounce) package very small new potatoes	340 g

- Brown pork chops in large skillet with a little oil. Pour gravy and milk or water into skillet and stir mixture around chops until it mixes well.
- Add new potatoes around chops and gravy. Place lid on skillet and simmer on low to medium heat for about 15 minutes or until potatoes are tender.

TIP: *The (18 ounce/510 g) package pork chops will give you about 5 to 6 chops if they are the average size.*

■

Coconut-Orange Salad

1 (6 ounce) package orange gelatin	168 g
1 pint vanilla ice cream, softened	.5 kg
½ cup flaked coconut	120 ml
1 (11 ounce) can mandarin oranges, drained	312 g

- Dissolve gelatin in 1 cup (240 ml) boiling water. Cool slightly and fold in ice cream, coconut and oranges. Pour into 7 x 11-inch (18 x 28 cm) dish and refrigerate.

Oriental Night

Chop Chop Pork

6 boneless or loin pork chops
1 (14 ounce) can chicken broth   396 g
2 (1 ounce) packages dry onion gravy mix   2 (28 g)
4 red potatoes, sliced

- Seasoned chops with a little salt and pepper and brown in large skillet with a little oil. Combine chicken broth and gravy mix. Add potatoes to skillet with pork chops and cover with gravy mixture.
- Heat to boil, cover and simmer 45 minutes or until pork chops and potatoes are fork-tender.

■

Spinach Salad Oriental

1 (10 ounce) package fresh spinach   280 g
2 eggs, hard-boiled, sliced
1 (14 ounce) can bean sprouts, drained   396 g
1 (8 ounce) can water chestnuts, chopped   227 g

- Combine all ingredients and top with dressing below.

■

Dressing:

¾ cup olive oil   180 ml
⅓ cup sugar   80 ml
¼ cup ketchup   60 ml
3 tablespoons red wine vinegar   45 ml

- Combine all ingredients, mix well and use some of dressing for salad. (You will have some leftover.)

■ ■ ■

Can't Get Much Easier Than This

Easy Baked Chops

4 (½-1 inch) pork chops	4 (1.2 cm)
1 - 2 tablespoons onion soup mix	15 ml
2 tablespoons French salad dressing	30 ml

- Preheat oven to 350° (176° C). Brown pork chops on both sides in large skillet with a little oil. Sprinkle soup mix over top.
- Pour in salad dressing and ¼ cup (60 ml) cup water. Cover and bake for about 1 hour.

■

Posh Squash

8 medium yellow squash, sliced	
½ green bell pepper, seeded, chopped	
1 small onion, chopped	
1 (8 ounce) package Mexican processed cheese, cubed	227 g

- Combine squash, bell pepper and onion in large saucepan and just barely cover with water. Cook just until tender, about 10 to 15 minutes.
- Drain well, add cheese and stir until cheese melts. Pour into buttered 2-quart (2 L) baking dish. Bake at 350° (176° C) for 15 minutes.

■ ■ ■

Curried Chops

Curried-Orange Pork Chops

¾ teaspoon curry powder, divided	4 ml
½ teaspoon paprika	2 ml
4 (½-inch) thick center-cut boneless pork chops	4 (1.2 cm)
½ cup orange marmalade	120 ml
1 heaping teaspoon prepared horseradish	5 ml
1 teaspoon balsamic vinegar	5 ml

- Combine ¼ teaspoon (1 ml) curry powder, paprika and ½ teaspoon (2 ml) salt and sprinkle over pork chops. Place chops in skillet on medium-high heat and cook 5 minutes on each side. Transfer chops to plate.
- In same skillet, combine remaining ½ teaspoon (2 ml) curry, marmalade, horseradish and vinegar. Cook for 1 minute.
- When serving, spoon sauce over pork chops. Serve over hot cooked rice or couscous.

■

Green Beans and Mushrooms

¼ cup (½ stick) butter	60 ml
1 small onion, chopped	
1 (8 ounce) carton fresh shiitake mushrooms, sliced	227 g
2 pounds fresh green beans, trimmed	1 kg
¾ cup chicken broth	180 ml

- In saucepan, melt half butter and saute onion and mushrooms and transfer to small bowl.
- In same saucepan, melt remaining butter and toss with green beans. Pour chicken broth over beans and bring to a boil.
- Reduce heat, cover and simmer until beans are tender-crisp. Stir in mushroom mixture.

■ ■ ■

I'm Stuffed

Stuffed Pork Chops

4 (¾-inch) thick boneless center-cut pork chops	4 (1.8 cm)

Stuffing:

2 slices rye bread, diced	
⅓ cup chopped onion	80 ml
⅓ cup chopped celery	80 ml
⅓ cup dried apples, diced	80 ml
⅓ cup chicken broth	80 ml

- Preheat oven to 400° (204° C). Make 1-inch (2.5 cm) wide slit on side of each chop and insert knife blade to other side, but not through pork chop. Sweep knife back and forth and carefully cut pocket opening larger.
- In bowl, combine rye bread pieces, onion, celery, apples and broth and mix well. Stuff chops with all the stuffing mixture.
- Place chops in heavy skillet with a little oil and saute each chop about 3 minutes on each side. Transfer to non-stick baking dish and bake uncovered for10 minutes.

■

Almond Green Beans

⅓ cup slivered almonds	80 ml
¼ cup (½ stick) butter	60 ml
¾ teaspoon garlic salt	4 ml
3 tablespoons lemon juice	45 ml
2 (16 ounce) cans French-style green beans	2 (.5 kg)

- In saucepan, cook almonds in butter, garlic salt and lemon juice until slightly golden brown.
- Add drained green beans to almonds and heat.

■ ■ ■

Holy Smoke

Smoky Grilled Pork Chops

1 cup mayonnaise (not light)	240 ml
2 tablespoons lime juice	30 ml
1 teaspoon ground cilantro	5 ml
1 teaspoon chili powder	5 ml
2 teaspoons minced garlic	10 ml
8 (1-inch) thick bone-in, pork chops	8 (2.5 cm)

- Combine mayonnaise, lime juice, cilantro, chili powder and garlic and mix. Set ½ cup (120 ml) aside.
- Grill or broil pork chops 6 minutes on each side and brush with ½ cup (120 ml) sauce. Serve remaining ½ cup (120 ml) sauce with chops.

■

Artichoke Fettuccine

1 (12 ounce) package fettuccine	340 g
1 (14 ounce) can artichoke hearts, drained, chopped	396 g
1 (10 ounce) box frozen green peas, thawed	280 g
1 (16 ounce) jar alfredo sauce	.5 kg
2 heaping tablespoons crumbled blue cheese	30 ml

- Cook fettuccine according to package directions. Drain and place in serving bowl to keep warm.
- In large saucepan, heat artichoke hearts, peas and alfredo sauce and stir well. Spoon into bowl with fettuccine and toss. Sprinkle with blue cheese and serve hot.

■ ■ ■

Easy Easy

Skillet Pork Chops

⅔ cup baking mix	160 ml
½ cup crushed saltine crackers	120 ml
1 egg	
6 boneless (½-inch) thick pork chops	6 (1.2 cm)

- In shallow bowl, combine baking mix, crushed crackers and a generous amount of salt and pepper. In another shallow bowl, beat egg with 2 tablespoons (30 ml) water.
- Heat skillet with small amount of oil. Dip each pork chop in egg mixture and then in cracker mixture. Place in heated skillet and cook 8 to 10 minutes on each side.

■

Speedy Zucchini and Fettuccine

1 (9 ounce) package refrigerated fresh fettuccine	255 g
⅓ cup extra-virgin olive oil, divided	80 ml
1 tablespoon minced garlic	15 ml
4 small zucchini, grated	
1 tablespoon lemon juice	15 ml
½ cup pine nuts, toasted	120 ml
⅓ cup grated parmesan cheese	80 ml

- Cook fettuccine according to package directions, drain and place in serving bowl. Heat large skillet over high heat and add 2 tablespoons (30 ml) oil, garlic and zucchini. Saute for 1 minute.
- Add zucchini mixture to pasta. Add lemon juice, pine nuts and salt and pepper to taste. Stir in remaining olive oil and toss to combine. To serve, sprinkle parmesan cheese over top of dish.

■ ■ ■

Great Chops

Savory Pork Chops

6 (½-inch) thick pork chops	6 (1.2 cm)
1 tablespoon soy sauce	15 ml
½ cup thick-and-chunky salsa	120 ml
½ cup honey	120 ml
Hot cooked rice	

- Preheat oven to 325° (162° C). In large skillet, brown pork chops in a little oil. Place browned chops in sprayed 9 x 13-inch (23 x 33 cm) baking pan.
- In small bowl, combine soy sauce, salsa, honey and S! cup (80 ml) water. Pour mixture over pork chops. Cover with foil and bake 50 minutes. Serve over hot cooked rice

■

Cabbage-Carrot Slaw

1 (10 ounce) package slaw mix	280 g
1 (16 ounce) package shredded carrots	.5 kg
2 delicious apples, diced	
1 cup Craisins® (dried cranberries)	240 ml
⅔ cup chopped walnuts	160 ml
1 (8 ounce) bottle poppy seed salad dressing	227 g

- In salad bowl, combine slaw mix, carrots, apples, Craisins® and walnuts. Toss with poppy seed dressing and chill.

■ ■ ■

Chops Away

Potato-Pork Chops

6 boneless loin pork chops	
1 (14 ounce) can chicken broth	396 g
2 (1 ounce) packets dry onion gravy mix	2 (28 g)
6 red potatoes, thickly sliced	

- Season pork chops with a little black pepper and brown in large skillet with a little oil. Combine chicken broth, gravy mix and ¾ cup (180 ml) water. Add potatoes to skillet with pork chops and cover with gravy mixture.

- Heat to a boil, reduce heat, cover and simmer 45 minutes or until pork chops and potatoes are fork-tender.

■

Green Caesar Bake

2 pounds fresh green beans with ends snapped	1 kg
1 (6 ounce) package garlic-flavored croutons, lightly crushed, divided	168 g
1½ cups bottled creamy Caesar-style salad dressing	360 ml
⅓ cup grated parmesan cheese	80 ml
1 tablespoon lemon juice	15 ml

- Preheat oven to 350° (176° C). In saucepan with salted water bring to boil, add green beans and cook about 8 minutes or just until tender. Drain and rinse with cold water.

- Transfer beans to large bowl and stir in 1 cup (240 ml) croutons, salad dressing, cheese and lemon juice. Spoon into sprayed 7 x 11-inch (18 x 28 cm) baking dish. Top with remaining croutons and bake 30 minutes or until top is golden brown.

Ginger Chops

Pork Chops with Ginger-Soy Sauce

¾ cup chili sauce	180 ml
2 teaspoons minced garlic	10 ml
1 tablespoon minced fresh ginger	15 ml
2 tablespoons Worcestershire sauce	30 ml
1 large egg, beaten	
½ cup seasoned breadcrumbs	120 ml
2 tablespoons oil	30 ml
4 (¾-inch) thick boneless pork chops	4 (1.8 cm)

- In small bowl, combine chili sauce, garlic, ginger and Worcestershire and set aside for flavors to blend.
- Place egg with 1 tablespoon (15 ml) water, in shallow bowl. Place breadcrumbs in another shallow bowl. In skillet on medium heat, add oil. Dip each chop in beaten egg and dredge in breadcrumbs to coat well. Cook in skillet for 5 minutes on each side. Serve with ginger-soy sauce.

■

Italian Style Rice and Beans

1 (16 ounce) package frozen chopped onions and bell peppers	.5 kg
2 tablespoons olive oil	30 ml
1 (15 ounce) can Italian-stewed tomatoes	425 g
1 (15 ounce) can great northern beans, drained	425 g
1 cup uncooked instant rice	

- In large saucepan, saute onions and bell peppers in oil. Add tomatoes, beans, ½ cup (120 ml) water and rice and stir well.
- Over medium heat, cover and cook about 3 minutes. Uncover and continue cooking another 3 minutes, stirring once.

■ ■ ■

Salsa Chops

Pork Chops with Black Bean Salsa

2 teaspoons chili powder	10 ml
½ teaspoon seasoned salt	2 ml
2 tablespoons vegetable oil	30 ml
6 thin-cut, boneless pork chops	

Black Bean Salsa:

1 (15 ounce) can black beans, rinsed, drained	425 g
1 (24 ounce) refrigerated citrus fruit, drained	680 g
1 ripe avocado, sliced	
⅔ cup Italian salad dressing	160 ml

- Combine chili powder and seasoned salt. Rub oil over pork chops, sprinkle chili powder mixture over chops and rub into meat. Place in skillet over medium heat and cook pork chops about 5 minutes on both sides.
- For salsa, combine beans, fruit and avocado and toss with salad dressing. Serve with pork chops.

■

Zucchini and Creamy Penne

4 medium zucchini, sliced	
2 tablespoons olive oil, divided	30 ml
1 (16 ounce) package penne pasta	.5 kg
1 (8 ounce) carton whipping cream	227 g
6 ounces crumbled goat cheese	168 g

- In saucepan, cook zucchini in a little salted water, drain and add olive oil. Cook penne according to package directions. Drain and add remaining olive oil.
- While zucchini and pasta are still hot, combine ingredients, stir in whipping cream and goat cheese and toss. Serve hot.

■ ■ ■

Nice Combination

Parmesan-Topped Pork Chops

½ cup grated parmesan cheese	120 ml
⅔ cup Italian-seasoned dried breadcrumbs	160 ml
1 egg	
4 - 6 thin-cut pork chops	

- In shallow bowl, combine cheese and dried breadcrumbs. Beat egg with 1 teaspoon (5 ml) water on shallow plate.
- Dip each pork chop in beaten egg and breadcrumb mixture. Cook over medium-high heat, in skillet with a little oil, for about 5 minutes on each side or until light golden brown.

■

Pecan-Mushroom Rice

1½ cups whole pecans	360 ml
1½ cups uncooked instant rice	360 ml
1 (14 ounce) can chicken broth	396 g
¼ cup (½ stick) butter	60 ml
2 (8 ounce) cans whole mushrooms, drained	2 (227 g)
2 teaspoons prepared, minced garlic	10 ml
3 cups baby spinach leaves, stems removed	710 ml
½ cup grated parmesan cheese	120 ml

- In large saucepan, cook and stir pecans over medium heat for 5 minutes. Remove from pan and cool slightly.
- Cook rice in chicken broth and butter according to package directions. Gently stir in mushrooms, garlic, spinach, cheese and pecans. Serve immediately.

Tuna Special

Tuna-Tomato Bowl

2 tablespoons olive oil	30 ml
1 teaspoon minced garlic	5 ml
¼ teaspoon cayenne pepper	1 ml
2 teaspoons dried basil	10 ml
1 (15 ounce) can stewed tomatoes	425 g
1 (12 ounce) can water-packed tuna, drained	340 g
¾ cup pitted green olives, sliced	180 ml
¼ cup drained capers	60 ml
1 cup favorite pasta, cooked	240 ml

- In saucepan, heat olive oil and add garlic, cayenne pepper and basil; cook on low heat for 2 minutes. Add tomatoes and bring to a boil, reduce heat and simmer 20 minutes.
- In bowl, combine tuna, olives, capers, pasta and salt to taste. Stir in oil-tomato sauce and toss. Serve immediately.

■

Seasoned Breadsticks

1 (11 ounce) tube refrigerated breadsticks	312 g
¼ cup (½ stick) butter, melted	60 ml
2 tablespoons prepared pesto	30 ml
¼ teaspoon garlic powder	1 ml
3 tablespoons grated parmesan cheese	45 ml

- Preheat oven to 375° (190° C). Separate breadsticks and place on ungreased baking pan. Combine melted butter, pesto and garlic powder and brush over breadsticks.
- Twist each breadstick 3 times. Sprinkle with parmesan cheese. Bake for about 12 minutes or until golden brown.

■ ■ ■

Stuffed Tomatoes

Tuna-Stuffed Tomatoes

4 large tomatoes	
2 (6 ounce) cans white meat tuna, drained	2 (168 g)
2 cups chopped celery	480 ml
½ cup chopped cashews	120 ml
1 small zucchini with peel, chopped	
½ - ⅔ cup mayonnaise	120 ml

- Cut thin slice off top of each tomato, scoop out pulp and discard. Turn tomatoes over on paper towels to drain.
- Combine tuna, celery, cashews and zucchini and mix well. Add ½ cup (120 ml) mayonnaise; add more if needed. Spoon into hollowed tomatoes and chill.

■

Veggie Quiche

½ (15 ounce) package ready-to-bake piecrust	½ (425 g)
1 (24 ounce) bag frozen broccoli, carrots, cauliflower in cheese sauce, thawed	680 g
¼ cup (½ stick) butter, melted	60 ml
1 (15 ounce) carton cheese-chive egg beaters	425 g

- Preheat oven to 400° (204° C). Place 1 piecrust in sprayed 9-inch (23 cm) pie plate. Turn edges under and crimp. Prick crust in 4 or 5 places and bake for 12 minutes or until edges are light brown.
- Microwave vegetables and cheese sauce according to package directions. In bowl combine vegetables, melted butter and egg beaters and pour into baked crust.
- Bake 15 minutes, then reduce heat to 350° (176° C) and continue baking another 20 minutes or until center is set

■ ■ ■

Good Ole Stand-by

Tuna Casserole

1 (7 ounce) package elbow macaroni	198 g
1 (8 ounce) package shredded processed cheese	227 g
2 (6 ounce) cans tuna, drained	2 (168 g)
1 (10 ounce) can cream of celery soup	280 g
1 cup milk	240 ml

- Preheat oven to 350° (176° C). Cook macaroni according to package directions. Drain well, add cheese and stir until cheese melts.
- Add tuna, celery soup and milk and continue stirring. Spoon into greased 7 x 11-inch (18 x 28 cm) baking dish. Cover and bake 35 minutes or until bubbly.

■

Emergency Cheesecake

1 (8 ounce) package cream cheese, softened	227 g
1 (14 ounce) sweetened condensed milk	396 g
½ cup lemon juice	120 ml
1 teaspoon vanilla	5 ml
1 (6 ounce) graham cracker piecrust	168 g

- Blend all ingredients with mixer. Pour into graham cracker crust and refrigerate. Top with cherry pie filling, if desired.

■ ■ ■

Thai It Up

Thai Peanut and Noodles

1 (5.5 ounce) box Thai stir-fry rice noodles	155 g
1 pound peeled, veined shrimp	.5 kg
1 (10 ounce) package frozen broccoli florets, thawed	280 g
½ cup peanuts	120 ml

- In saucepan on high heat bring 3 cups (710 ml) water to a boil and stir in noodles. Turn heat off and let noodles soak about 5 minutes. Drain and rinse in cold water.

- In skillet with a little oil, saute shrimp and broccoli about 8 minutes or just until shrimp is pink. Add softened noodles, seasoning packet and peanuts.

TIP: *If noodles are still to firm, add 1 tablespoon (15 ml) water and stir-fry until tender. There are chopped peanuts in seasoning, but this is better if you add more peanuts.*

■

Greens and Fruit

1 (10 ounce) package spring salad greens	280 g
1 (11 ounce) can mandarin oranges, drained	312 g
¼ cup sliced almonds	60 ml
1 cup halved, green seedless grapes	240 ml
1 (8 ounce) raspberry vinaigrette salad dressing	227 g
¼ cup precooked bacon bits	60 ml

- In salad bowl, combine salad greens, oranges, almonds and grapes. Toss with half raspberry vinaigrette salad dressing, adding more if needed. Sprinkle with bacon bits.

Yum Yum Shrimp

Shrimp and Rice Casserole

2 cups instant rice	480 ml
1½ pounds frozen cooked shrimp	.7 kg
1 (10 ounce) carton alfredo sauce	280 g
1 (4 ounce) can chopped pimento, drained	114 g
4 fresh green onions with tops, chopped	
1 (8 ounce) package shredded cheddar cheese, divided	227 g

- In saucepan, cook rice according to package directions and place in sprayed 9 x 13-inch (23 x 33 cm) baking dish. Thaw shrimp in colander under cold running water, drain well and remove tails. Set aside.

- In saucepan on medium heat, combine alfredo sauce, pimento and green onions. Stir in shrimp and spoon mixture over rice. Cover with about half cheese and bake about 15 minutes. Remove from oven and sprinkle remaining cheese on top and return to oven for 5 minutes.

TIP: *Thawing shrimp under running water is better than thawing in refrigerator.*

■

Orange-Glazed Carrots

2 (16 ounce) packages peeled baby carrots	2 (.5 kg)
¼ cup (½ stick) butter, melted	60 ml
½ cup orange marmalade	120 ml
½ teaspoon ground ginger	2 ml

- Preheat oven to 350° (176 C). Place carrots in large glass baking dish and pour melted butter over top and toss. Cover and bake for 30 minutes.

- Stir in marmalade and ginger and bake another 30 minutes.

■ ■ ■

A Little Bit Different

Shrimp and Chicken Curry

2 (10 ounce) cans cream of chicken soup	2 (280 g)
⅓ cup milk	80 ml
1½ teaspoons curry powder	7 ml
1 (12 ounce) can chicken breast, drained	340 g
2 (6 ounce) cans shrimp, drained	2 (168 g)
Hot cooked rice	

- In saucepan, heat soup, milk and curry powder. Stir in chicken pieces and shrimp. Heat, stirring constantly, until mixture heats thoroughly.
- Serve over hot cooked rice.

■

Potatoes Italian-Style

1 (22 ounce) package frozen mashed potatoes, thawed	624 g
1 (1 pint) half-and-half cream	.5 kg
1½ cups grated parmesan cheese, divided	360 ml
1 (8 ounce) jar traditional basil pesto, divided	227 g

- Place mashed potatoes, cream and ample salt and pepper in microwave-safe bowl. Microwave on HIGH for about 10 minutes, stir once and cook until potatoes are hot. Stir in half of cheese and mix well.
- Spread half of potato-cheese mixture into 7 x 11-inch (18 x 28 cm) sprayed baking dish and spread T! cup (160 ml) basil pesto on top. (Chill remaining pesto to store.)
- Spoon remaining potato mixture on top of pesto. Sprinkle remaining parmesan cheese over top and return to microwave for another 2 minutes.

■ ■ ■

Easy Newburg

Shrimp Newburg

2 (10 ounce) can cream of shrimp soup	2 (280 g)
1 teaspoon seafood seasoning	5ml
1 (1 pound) frozen cooked salad shrimp, thawed	.5 kg
Hot cooked rice	

- Combine soup, ¼ cup (60 ml) water and seafood seasoning in saucepan. Bring to a boil, reduce heat and cook for 3 minutes. Stir in shrimp. Heat thoroughly and serve over hot white rice.

Spinach-Pecan Salad

1 (10 ounce) package baby spinach	280 g
2 eggs, hard-boiled, sliced	
½ cup pecans, toasted	120 ml
1 (6 ounce) package cooked bacon, crumbled	168 g
¼ cup crumbled blue cheese	60 ml
1 (8 ounce) bottle Italian salad dressing	227 g

- In salad bowl, combine spinach, sliced eggs, pecans, bacon and blue cheese and toss. Drizzle with salad dressing.

Great Fish

Alfredo Salmon and Noodles

3 cups uncooked medium egg noodles	710 ml
1 (16 ounce) package frozen broccoli florets, thawed	.5 kg
1 cup prepared alfredo sauce	240 ml
1 (15 ounce) can salmon, drained, boned, flaked	425 g

- In large saucepan, cook noodles according to package directions and add broccoli last 5 minutes of cooking. (Discard some of broccoli stems.) Drain.
- Stir in alfredo sauce and salmon and cook on low heat, stirring occasionally, until mixture heats thoroughly. Spoon into serving bowl.

■

Pear and Goat Cheese Salad

1 (10 ounce) package baby salad greens	280 g
¾ cup crumbled goat cheese	180 ml
2 pears, peeled, sliced	
½ cup balsamic vinaigrette salad dressing	120 ml
½ cup coarsely chopped walnuts	120 ml

- In salad bowl, combine salad greens, cheese and pear slices and toss with salad dressing. Sprinkle walnuts over top of salad to serve.

■ ■ ■

Catch Of The Night

Fish and Chips

1 cup mayonnaise	240 ml
1 lime	
3 - 4 fish fillets, rinsed, dried	
1½ cups crushed corn chips	360 ml

- Preheat oven to 425° (220° C). Mix mayonnaise and 2 tablespoons (30 ml) lime juice. Spread on both sides of fish fillets.
- Place crushed corn chips on wax paper and dredge both sides of fish in chips. Shake off excess chips.
- Place fillets on foil-covered baking sheet and bake for 15 minutes or until fish flakes. Serve with lime wedges.

■

Baked Beans

2 (15 ounce) cans pork and beans,	
slightly drained	2 (425 g)
½ onion, finely chopped	
⅔ cup packed brown sugar	160 ml
¼ cup chili sauce	60 ml
1 tablespoon Worcestershire sauce	15 ml
2 strips bacon	

- In bowl, combine beans, onion, brown sugar, chili sauce and Worcestershire.
- Pour into buttered 2-quart (2 L) baking dish and place bacon strips over bean mixture. Bake uncovered at 325° (162° C) for 50 minutes.

■ ■ ■

Sunday Special

Creamed Shrimp-Over-Rice

3 (10 ounce) cans cream of shrimp soup	3 (280 g)
1 (8 ounce) carton sour cream	227 g
1½ teaspoons curry powder	7 ml
1 (12 ounce) package frozen salad shrimp, thawed	340 g
1 (3.5 ounce box) boil-in-bag rice	100 g

- Combine soup, sour cream, curry powder, shrimp and ½ cup (120 ml) water in double boiler. Heat while stirring constantly.
- Cook both packets of rice according to package directions and place on serving platter. Spoon shrimp mixture over rice.

■

Sunday Special Apple Salad

1 (20 ounce) can crushed pineapple with juice	567 g
⅔ cup sugar	160 ml
1 tablespoon flour	15 ml
1 tablespoon white vinegar	15 ml
1 (12 ounce) carton whipped topping	340 g
3 red delicious apples with peeled, diced	
1 (10 ounce) package miniature marshmallows	280 g
½ cup roasted peanuts	120 ml

- Drain pineapple, save juice and set pineapple aside. In saucepan, combine juice, sugar, flour and vinegar, mix well.
- Place on medium heat and cook, stirring constantly, until mixture thickens. Set aside to cool.
- Transfer to large salad bowl and fold in whipped topping, pineapple, diced apples and marshmallows and chill. To serve, sprinkle peanuts over top of salad.

Extra Special

Extra-Special Fried Fish

1 (16 ounce) package frozen, cooked, batter-dipped fried fish	.5 kg
¾ cup chili sauce	180 ml
1 bunch fresh green onions, chopped	
1 cup shredded cheddar cheese	240 ml

- Preheat oven to 325° (162° C). Arrange fish in sprayed 9 x 13-inch (23 x 33 cm) glass baking dish and bake about 20 minutes or just until fish heats thoroughly.
- In saucepan, heat chili sauce and spoon over each piece of fish. Top with chopped green onions and cheddar cheese. Serve fish right from baking dish.

■

A Different Macaroni

1 (8 ounce) package shell macaroni	227 g
½ cup whipping cream	120 ml
8 ounces shredded gorgonzola cheese	227 g
1 (10 ounce) package frozen green peas, thawed	280 g
2 cups cubed ham	480 ml

- Cook macaroni according to package directions and drain. Stir in cream and gorgonzola cheese and stir until cheese melts.
- Fold in peas and ham and cook on low heat, stirring constantly, for 5 minutes or until mixture is thoroughly hot. Spoon into serving bowl and serve hot.

■ ■ ■

BREAKFAST
SUPPERS

Breakfast Any Time

Breakfast Frittata

2 medium zucchini, diced, dried	
1 cup finely diced fresh mushrooms	240 ml
2 ripe avocados, peeled, cubed	
5 eggs	
1½ cups shredded Swiss cheese	360 ml

- Cook zucchini and mushrooms in large skillet with a little oil over medium heat for 4 to 5 minutes or just until tender. Remove from heat and sprinkle with a little salt and pepper.
- Place cubed avocado over top of vegetable mixture. Beat eggs and about 1 cup (240 ml) water or milk until frothy and pour over ingredients in skillet.
- Return skillet to medium heat, cover and cook 5 minutes or until eggs set. Top with cheese, cover and cook 1 minute more or just until cheese melts. Cut in wedges to serve.

■

Hot Biscuits

1⅓ cups self-rising flour	320 ml
1 (8 ounce) carton whipping cream	227 g
2 tablespoons sugar	30 ml
Butter	

- Combine all ingredients and stir until they blend. Drop biscuits by teaspoon onto greased baking sheet.
- Bake at 400° (204° C) for about 10 minutes or until light brown. Serve with plain or flavored butters.

Light, Easy and So Good

Crabmeat Quiche

3 eggs, beaten	
1 (8 ounce) carton sour cream	227 g
1 (6 ounce) can crabmeat, rinsed	168 g
½ cup grated Swiss cheese	120 ml
1 (9-inch) unbaked pie shell	23 cm

- Combine eggs and sour cream in bowl. Blend in crabmeat and cheese and add a little garlic, salt and pepper.
- Pour into pie shell and bake at 350° (176° C) for 35 minutes.

■

Crunchy Breadsticks

1 (8 count) package hot dog buns	
1 cup (2 sticks) butter, melted	240 ml
Garlic powder	
Paprika	

- Preheat oven to 225° (107° C). Slice each bun in half lengthwise.
- Use pastry brush to butter all breadsticks and sprinkle a little garlic powder and a couple sprinkles of paprika on each.
- Place on baking sheet and bake for 45 minutes.

■

Melon Boats

2 cantaloupes, chilled	
4 cups red and green seedless grapes, chilled	960 ml
1 cup mayonnaise	240 ml
⅓ cup frozen concentrated orange juice	80 ml

- Prepare each melon in 6 lengthwise sections and remove seeds and peel. Place on separate salad plates on lettuce leaves.
- Heap grapes over and around cantaloupe slices.
- Combine mayonnaise and juice concentrate and mix well. Ladle over fruit.

■ ■ ■

Light and Fancy

Brunch Bake

1 pound hot sausage, cooked, crumbled	.5 kg
1 cup grated cheddar cheese	240 ml
1 cup biscuit mix	240 ml
5 eggs, slightly beaten	
2 cups milk	480 ml

- Place sausage in sprayed 9 x 13-inch (23 x 33 cm) baking dish. sprinkle with cheese.
- In mixing bowl, combine biscuit mix, a little salt and eggs; beat well. Add milk and stir until fairly smooth. Pour over sausage mixture.
- Bake covered at 350° (176° C) for 35 minutes. You can mix this up the night before cooking. Refrigerate. To cook the next morning, add 5 minutes to cooking time.

■

Cherry Tomato Salad

2 tablespoons red-wine vinegar	30 ml
2 tablespoons olive oil	30 ml
2 teaspoons sugar	10 ml
2 pints cherry tomatoes, halved	1 kg
1 bunch fresh green onions, chopped	
1 small cucumber, peeled, chopped	

- Combine vinegar, olive oil, sugar, 1 teaspoon (5 ml) salt and ½ teaspoon (2 ml) pepper and mix well.
- In salad bowl, combine tomato halves, green onions and cucumber, toss with dressing and chill.

A Little Bit Southern

Fancy French-Onion Pie

2 (3 ounce) cans fried onions rings	2 (84 g)
1 (9 inch) piecrust	23 cm
1½ cups milk	360 ml
4 eggs, beaten	
1 cup shredded cheddar cheese	240 ml

- Preheat oven to 425° (220° C). Crumble onion rings and sprinkle over piecrust. Pour milk into beaten eggs and mix. Pour mixture into piecrust over onion rings and spread cheese on top.
- Bake for 15 minutes. Reduce heat to 350° (176°) and bake additional 15 to 20 minutes or until center sets. Cool slightly before slicing and serving.

■

Creamy Grits

3 pints half-and half-cream	1.3 kg
½ teaspoon garlic powder	2 ml
½ teaspoon hot sauce	2 ml
1½ cups uncooked grits	360 ml
2 (3 ounce) packages cream cheese	2 (84 g

- In large saucepan combine half-and-half, garlic powder, hot sauce and 1 teaspoon (5 ml) salt. Bring to a boil and gradually stir in grits.
- Reduce heat to low and simmer 6 minutes or until mixture thickens; stir occasionally. Add cream cheese and stir until it melts. Serve hot.

Presto Eggs

Easy Baked Eggs Presto

6 teaspoons butter, melted	30 ml
6 large eggs	
6 teaspoons shredded cheddar cheese	30 ml
6 teaspoons ready-cooked bacon	30 ml

- Pour 1 teaspoon (5 ml) butter into each cup of 6-cup (1.5 L) muffin pan. Carefully break 1 egg into each cup and top with 1 teaspoon (5 ml) cheese for each cup.
- Sprinkle bacon on top and season with a little salt and pepper.

TIP: *If you want a little "kick", add a few drops of hot sauce or Worcestershire sauce.*

■

Orange-French Toast

1 egg, beaten	
½ cup orange juice	120 ml
5 slices raisin bread	
1 cup crushed graham crackers	240 ml
¼ cup (½ stick) butter	60 ml

- Combine egg and orange juice and dip slices of bread in egg mixture. Dip in graham cracker crumbs and fry in butter until light brown.

■ ■ ■

Sunday Night Eggs

Sunday Night Eggs

2 tablespoons butter, melted	30 ml
¾ cup shredded Swiss cheese, divided	180 ml
5 eggs	
2 tablespoons half-and-cream	30 ml
¼ cup milk	60 ml

- Preheat oven to 350° (176°). Pour butter into small baking dish and turn dish from side to side to spread butter. Sprinkle half of cheese over butter.
- Carefully crack eggs and pour into dish without breaking yolks. Pour cream and milk around outside of eggs to keep from breaking yolks. Season with a little salt and pepper and sprinkle remaining cheese over top.
- Bake for about 10 minutes or until whites set and cheese melts.

■

Easy Way to Cook Bacon

1 pound bacon	.5 kg

- Preheat oven to 400° (204° C). Place slices of bacon on rack of roasting pan.
- Bake for 20 to 30 minutes or until crisp. Remove bacon with tongs and discard bacon drippings.

■ ■ ■

Slide Out Of The Rain

Easy Omelet

2 tablespoons butter	30 ml
4 - 5 eggs	
⅓ cup shredded cheddar cheese	80 ml

- Melt butter in 10-inch (25 cm) skillet over medium heat. While butter melts, whisk together eggs and ¼ teaspoon (1 ml) salt. Pour eggs into skillet and stir gently until they begin to set.

- Spread eggs evenly in pan and sprinkle with cheese. Reduce heat and cook until omelet just sets. Hold skillet over serving plate, tilt skillet until omelet slides out and almost half touches plate. Immediately turn skillet upside down to make omelet fold over itself. Serve immediately.

■

Holiday Rolls

1 (18 roll) package frozen dinner rolls, thawed	
¼ cup (½ stick) butter, melted	60 ml
2 cups finely chopped fresh cranberries	480 ml
½ cup sugar	120 ml

- Preheat oven to 350° (176° C). Spray counter with cooking spray. Spread rolls into 10 x 16-inch (25 x 40 cm) rectangle and brush with melted butter.

- Combine cranberries and sugar and spread over rectangle and press down. Begin with longer side, roll dough up tightly and cut into 12 equal pieces. Place in sprayed muffin cups, cover with plastic wrap and let rise 30 minutes. Bake for 15 to 20 minutes and remove from pan.

TIP: *These rolls may be served hot with butter or cooled slightly and iced with 1 (16 ounce/.5 kg) carton prepared vanilla icing.*

■ ■ ■

Family Tradition

Biscuits and Sausage Gravy

This is about as down-home as you can get and it is every bit as good as you can imagine.

3 cups biscuit mix	710 ml
¾ cup milk	180 ml
½ pound pork sausage	227 g
2 tablespoons (¼ stick) butter	30 ml
⅓ cup flour	80 ml
3¼ cups milk	770 ml

- Preheat oven to 400° (204° C).
- Combine biscuit mix and milk and stir. Roll dough on floured wax paper to ¾-inch (1.8 cm) thickness and cut with biscuit cutter. Place on greased baking sheet.
- Bake for 12 to 15 minutes or until golden.
- For gravy, brown sausage, drain and reserve pan drippings in skillet. Set sausage aside.
- Add butter to drippings and melt. Add flour and cook 1 minute, stirring constantly.
- Gradually add milk, cook over medium heat, stirring constantly until mixture thickens. Stir in ½ teaspoon (2 ml) each of salt and pepper and sausage.
- Cook until hot and stir constantly. Serve sausage gravy over cooked biscuits.

Late Night Special Anytime

Huevos Rancheros

½ cup chopped onion	120 ml
½ teaspoon minced garlic	2 ml
3 tablespoons bacon drippings	45 ml
4 tomatoes, seeded, finely chopped, drained	
Minced jalapenos peppers to taste	
6 eggs	
6 fried tortillas	

- Saute onion and garlic in bacon drippings. Add tomatoes, peppers and ½ teaspoon (2 ml) salt.
- Cover and simmer for 10 minutes. Fry each egg and place one on each tortilla. Spoon sauce over each egg and serve.

■

Bacon Nibblers

1 (1 pound) package sliced bacon, room temperature	1 kg
1½ cups packed brown sugar	360 ml
1½ teaspoons dry mustard	7 ml

- Cut each slice of bacon in half. Combine brown sugar, dry mustard and about ¼ teaspoon (1 ml) pepper in shallow bowl.
- Dip each half slice of bacon in brown sugar mixture and press down to make ingredients stick to bacon. Place on baking sheet with sides.
- Bake at 325° (162° C) for 25 minutes, turning once, until bacon browns. Immediately remove with tongs to several layers of paper towels to drain. Bacon will harden and can be broken in pieces.

Dad's Best Meal

Corned Beef Hash-N-Eggs

1 (15 ounce) can corned beef hash	425 g
1 (11 ounce) can mexicorn, drained	312 g
4 eggs	
¾ cup chili sauce	180 ml

- Preheat oven to 375° (190° C). Spread corned beef hash in greased 9-inch (23 cm) pie pan and spoon corn over hash.
- With large spoon, make 4 depressions in corn and break 1 egg in each depression. Spoon chili sauce over top of eggs.
- Bake for 20 minutes or until eggs set.

■

Garlic-Flavored Biscuits

5 cups biscuit mix	1.3 L
1 cup shredded cheddar cheese	240 ml
1 (14 ounce) can chicken broth with roasted garlic	396 g

- Mix all ingredients to form soft dough. Drop by heaping spoon-fuls onto greased baking sheet.
- Bake at 425° (220° C) for 10 minutes or until light brown.

■ ■ ■

Bedtime Story

Breakfast-Ready Oatmeal

1½ cups uncooked oatmeal	360 ml
3½ cups milk	830 ml
½ cup chopped pecans	120 ml
⅓ cup packed brown sugar	80 ml

- In saucepan, cook oats, milk, pecans, brown sugar and a dash of salt over medium heat. Bring to a boil, lower heat and simmer for 6 minutes, stirring occasionally. Let stand several minutes before serving. Serve with buttered toast.

■

Sausage Bites

¾ - 1 pound bacon slices	340 g
2 (8 ounce) package sausage links	2 (227 g)
1 cup packed brown sugar, divided	240 ml
½ teaspoon cinnamon	2 ml

- Preheat oven to 350° (176° C). Place foil in large baking dish. Cut each bacon strip in half and cut each sausage link in half. Wrap 1 piece bacon around each sausage half and secure with toothpick.
- Place brown sugar in shallow bowl and mix in cinnamon. Roll sausage rolls in brown sugar. (There will be some brown sugar left.)
- Place sausage rolls in baking dish, cover and refrigerate for several hours or overnight. When ready to bake, sprinkle several teaspoons brown sugar over each roll, bake for 35 minutes and turn once.

Cold Night, Warm Bowl

Cherry-Pecan Oatmeal

2 cups of your favorite cooked oatmeal	480 ml
½ cup dried cherries, chopped	120 ml
½ cup packed brown sugar	120 ml
¼ cup (½ stick) butter, softened	60 ml
½ teaspoon ground cinnamon	2 ml
½ cup chopped pecans, toasted	120 ml

- Cook your favorite oatmeal. Combine cherries, brown sugar, butter and cinnamon. Stir into cooked oatmeal.
- Spoon into individual serving bowls and sprinkle toasted pecans over top of each serving.

TIP: Toasting brings out the flavors of nuts and seeds. Place nuts on baking sheet and bake at 225° (107° C) for 10 minutes. Be careful not to burn them.

■

Cream Cheese Biscuits

1 (3 ounce) package cream cheese, softened	84 g
½ cup (1 stick) butter, softened	120 ml
1 cup self-rising flour	240 ml

- In mixing bowl beat cream cheese and butter together. Add flour and mix well. Roll out to ½-inch (1.2 cm) thickness and cut with small biscuit cutter or glass.
- Place on greased baking sheet and bake at 350° (176 C) for 20 minutes or until light brown.

Fast-Track Pancakes

No-Mess Oven Pancakes

⅔ cup flour	160 ml
⅔ cup milk	160 ml
¼ cup sugar	60 ml
5 large eggs, beaten	

- Preheat oven to 425° (220° C). Combine flour, milk, sugar and beaten eggs in mixing bowl. Place a little oil on large baking sheet and rub oil to cover whole surface of pan.
- Place in oven for 5 minutes to heat. Pour pancake mixture onto pan to make several pancakes. Bake about 18 minutes or until puffy and golden.
- Serve with maple syrup and fresh berries.

■

Toffee Milk Shake

1 pint vanilla ice cream, divided	.5 kg
¼ cup milk	60 ml
½ cup chocolate-coated toffee bits	120 ml

- Combine half ice cream and all milk in blender. Cover and blend until they combine. Add remaining ice cream.
- Cover and blend until desired consistency. Add toffee bits and process briefly with on/off pulse to mix.

Down-Home Pancakes

2 cups flour	480 ml
1 tablespoon sugar	15 ml
1 tablespoon baking powder	15 ml
2 eggs	
1½ - 2 cups milk, divided	360 ml
Vegetable oil	
Maple syrup	
½ cup melted butter	120 ml

- Combine flour, sugar, baking powder and ¼ teaspoon (1 ml) salt in large mixing bowl.
- In separate bowl, beat eggs and 1½ cups milk. Pour egg mixture into flour mixture and stir until smooth. If batter is too thick, add a little milk. There will be a few lumps in batter.
- Heat griddle and coat lightly with oil. Slowly pour circle of batter on griddle to equal desired size of pancake. After bubbles form on top and edges brown, gently flip pancake to cook other side. Serve immediately with warm syrup and melted butter.

Blueberry Pancakes: Wash and drain thoroughly about 1 cup (240 ml) fresh or frozen blueberries. (If blueberries are frozen, do not thaw before adding to pancake batter.) Stir into pancake batter gently and pour onto griddle or skillet.

Buttermilk Pancakes: Substitute buttermilk instead of milk. If batter is too thick, add just a little milk.

Tip: *To make buttermilk, mix 1 cup (240 ml) milk with 1 tablespoon (15 ml) lemon juice or vinegar and let milk set for about 10 minutes.*

Banana Pancakes: Slice 1 or 2 ripe bananas about ¼-inch (.6 cm) thick. When batter is poured onto griddle, place as many slices as desired on batter and lightly push bananas into batter. Cook slowly to make sure inside is firm.

TIP: *Other variations include apples, cranberries, coconut, bacon, ham and pecans.*

■ ■ ■

The Best Waffles Ever

Pecan Waffles

2 cups self-rising flour	480 ml
½ cup oil	120 ml
½ cup milk	120 ml
⅔ cup finely chopped pecans	160 ml

- Preheat waffle iron. In bowl, combine flour, oil and milk. Beat until they mix well. Stir in chopped pecans.
- Pour approximately ¾ cup (180 ml) batter into hot waffle iron and bake until brown and crispy.

■

Glazed Bacon

1 (1 pound) package bacon	.5 kg
⅓ cup packed brown sugar	80 ml
1 teaspoon flour	5 ml
½ cup finely chopped pecans	120 ml

- Arrange bacon slices close together, but not overlapping, on wire rack over drip pan.
- In bowl, combine brown sugar, flour and pecans and sprinkle evenly over bacon.
- Bake at 350° (176° C) for about 30 minutes. Drain on paper towels.

The Best Sunday Night Tradition

Light and Crispy Waffles

2 cups biscuit mix	480 ml
1 egg	
½ cup oil	120 ml
1⅓ cups club soda	320 ml

- Preheat waffle iron. Combine all ingredients in mixing bowl and stir by hand.
- Pour just enough batter to cover waffle iron, but not run over.

TIP: *To have waffles for a "company weekend", make all waffles in advance. Freeze separately on baking sheet and place in large baggies. To heat, warm at 350° (176° C) for about 10 minutes.*

■

Orange Slush

2 cups orange juice	480 ml
½ cup instant, non-fat dry milk	120 ml
¼ teaspoon almond extract	1 ml
8 ice cubes	

- Add all ingredients in blender and process on high until mixture combines and thickens. Serve immediately.

■ ■ ■

Flash In The Pan

Waffle Flash

2 eggs
1 cup milk   240 ml
½ teaspoon vanilla   2 ml
8 slices stale bread

- Heat waffle iron according to directions. Beat eggs, slowly add milk and vanilla and beat well.
- Remove crust from bread and butter both sides of bread.
- When waffle iron is ready, dip bread in egg mixture and place in waffle iron. Close lid and grill until light brown. Serve with syrup.

■

Coconut Bananas

4 bananas
4 tablespoons lemon juice   60 ml
1 (16 ounce) carton sour cream   .5 kg
1¼ cups flaked coconut   300 ml

- Cut bananas into fourths. Place lemon juice, sour cream and coconut in separate bowls.
- Dip bananas into lemon juice, roll in sour cream and coconut. Covered thoroughly.
- Place in covered bowl and refrigerate several hours or overnight.

Traditional Sunday Eggs

Creamy Eggs on Toast

¼ cup (½ stick) butter	60 ml
4 level tablespoons flour	60 ml
2 cups milk	480 ml
6 eggs, hard-boiled, sliced	

- Melt butter in skillet, stir in flour and add milk. Cook over medium heat and stir constantly until sauce thickens.

- Gently fold in egg slices. Serve over 6 slices toasted bread.

■

Treasure-Filled Apples

6 tart apples	
½ cup sugar	120 ml
¼ cup cinnamon candies	60 ml
¼ teaspoon ground cinnamon	1 ml

- Cut tops off apples and set tops aside. Core apples to within ½-inch (1.2 cm) of bottom stem. Place in greased 8-inch (20 cm) baking dish.

- Combine sugar, candies and cinnamon in bowl and spoon 2 tablespoons (30 ml) into each apple. Replace tops on apples.

- Spoon any remaining sugar mixture over apples. Bake, uncovered, at 350° (176° C) for 30 to 35 minutes or until apples are tender and baste occasionally.

Eggs: A Sunday Night Tradition

Eggs In A Basket

2 (15 ounce) cans corned beef hash	2 (425 g)
6 eggs	
¼ cup seasoned breadcrumbs	60 ml
Butter	

- Preheat oven to 325° (162° C). Grease 7 x 11-inch (18 x 28 cm) baking dish and spread hash evenly in dish. Press bottom of ½ cup (120 ml) measuring cup into hash to make 6 impressions.
- Break 1 egg into each impression. Sprinkle spoonful of breadcrumbs over each egg and top with dot of butter. Bake 20 to 25 minutes or until eggs are as firm as desired.

■

Filled Muffins

1 (18 ounce) box blueberry muffin mix with blueberries	510 g
1 egg	
⅓ cup red raspberry jam	80 ml
¼ cup sliced almonds	60 ml

- Rinse blueberries and drain. Combine muffin mix, egg and ½ cup (120 ml) water in bowl. Stir until ingredients are moist. Break up any lumps in mix.
- Place paper liners in 8 muffin cups. Fill cups half full of batter. Combine raspberry jam with blueberries.
- Spoon mixture on top of batter. Cover with remaining batter and sprinkle almonds on top. Bake at 375° (190° C) for about 18 minutes or until light brown.

Too Hot To Handle

Hot Cheese Melt

1 (12 ounce) can whole jalapeno peppers, drained	340 g
1 (15 ounce) can Mexican stewed tomatoes	425 g
2 (16 ounce) packages cubed processed cheese	2 (.5 kg)
4 slices bacon, cooked crisp, crumbled	

- Cut peppers in half and remove seeds. Chop peppers and place in bottom of 9-inch (23 cm) pie plate.
- Spoon stewed tomatoes over peppers and place cheese over tomatoes.
- Bake at 300° (148° C) for about 15 minutes or until cheese melts. Let cheese sit until room temperature. When ready to serve, sprinkle bacon over top.
- Serve with tortilla chips.

■

Purple Shakes

1 (6 ounce) can frozen grape juice concentrate	168 g
1 cup milk	240 ml
2½ cups vanilla ice cream	600 ml
2 tablespoons sugar, optional	30 ml

- Combine all ingredients in blender. Cover and blend at high speed for 30 seconds. Serve immediately.

Sticky Sunday

Sticky Pecan Rolls

1 (12 count) package brown-and-serve dinner rolls
4 tablespoons (½ stick) butter   **60 ml**
⅔ cup packed brown sugar   **160 ml**
24 pecan halves

- Place 1 roll in each of 12 well-greased muffin cups.
- Cut an "x" in top of each roll. Combine sugar and butter, melt and mix well. Spoon mixture over rolls.
- Tuck 2 pecan halves in "x" on each roll. Bake at 350° (176° C) for 50 minutes or until slightly brown.

■

Banana Split Float

2 ripe bananas, mashed
3 cups milk   **710 ml**
1 (10 ounce) package frozen sweetened
    strawberries, thawed   **280 g**
1½ pints chocolate ice cream, divided   **.7 kg**

- Place bananas in blender and add milk, strawberries and ½ pint (227 g) chocolate ice cream. Beat just until ingredients blend.
- Pour into tall, chilled glasses and top each with scoop of chocolate ice cream.

I'll Have Four!

Praline Toast

½ cup (1 stick) butter, softened	120 ml
1 cup packed brown sugar	240 ml
½ cup finely chopped pecans	120 ml
Bread slices	

- Combine butter, sugar and pecans. Spread on bread slices.
- Toast in broiler until brown and bubbly.

■

Apricot Bake

4 (15 ounce) cans apricot halves, drained, divided	4 (425 g)
1 (16 ounce) box light brown sugar, divided	.5 kg
2 cups round, buttery cracker crumbs, divided	480 ml
½ cup (1 stick) butter, sliced	120 ml

- Grease 9 x 13-inch (23 x 33 cm) baking dish and line with 2 cans drained apricots.
- Sprinkle half brown sugar and half cracker crumbs over apricots. Dot with half butter and repeat layers.
- Bake at 300° (148° C) for 1 hour.

Strawberry Breakfast

Croissant French Toast
with Strawberry Syrup

4 large day-old croissants	
¾ cup half-and-half cream	180 ml
2 large eggs	
1 teaspoon vanilla	5 ml
¼ cup (½ stick) butter	60 ml

- Slice croissants in half lengthwise. In shallow bowl, whisk together cream, eggs and vanilla. Heat 1 tablespoon (15 ml) butter at a time in large skillet.

- Dip croissant halves into egg mixture and coat well. Cook 4 croissant halves about 2 minutes each time. Turn and cook on both sides until light brown. Repeat with remaining butter and croissant halves.

Strawberry Syrup:

¾ cup sugar	180 ml
1 quart fresh strawberries, slices	1 L
¼ cup orange juice	60 ml

- In saucepan, combine all ingredients and let stand 30 minutes. Cook over low heat and stir occasionally for 5 to 8 minutes. Serve warm over Croissant Toast.

■

Breakfast Shake

1 banana , sliced	
1 mango, sliced	
1½ cups pineapple or orange juice, chilled	360 ml
1 (8 ounce) container vanilla yogurt	227 g

- Process banana, mango, juice and yogurt in blender until smooth. Stop to scrape down sides of blender when necessary. Serve immediately.

■ ■ ■

Cake For A Meal

Cinnamon-Cake Breakfast

⅔ cup packed brown sugar	160 ml
1 tablespoon grated orange peel	15 ml
2 (12 ounce) packages refrigerated cinnamon rolls	2 (340 g

- Preheat oven to 375° (190° C). In small bowl, combine brown sugar and orange peel. Cut rolls into quarters and coat each quarter with cooking spray.

- Dip in sugar-orange mixture, arrange evenly in sprayed 10-inch (25 cm) bundt pan and gently press down. Bake 35 minutes until light brown and about double in size. Cool slightly in pan.

- Invert serving plate on top of pan and with oven mitts, hold plate and pan together and invert. Remove pan. Spread icing from rolls unevenly over top of cake and serve warm.

■

Heavenly Eggs

Bread and butter
Mozzarella cheese slices
Eggs
Cooked bacon strips

- Preheat oven to 350° (176° C). Butter enough bread slices for each person and place butter-side down in baking dish. Place cheese slice over bread.

- Separate 1 egg for each slice of bread. Add salt to taste to the whites and beat until stiff. Pile egg whites on cheese and make nest in top. Slip 1 egg yolk into each nest and bake for 20 minutes.

- Cut bacon slices in half and criss-cross halves over each egg. Serve immediately.

■ ■ ■

Parlez Vous Francaise?

French Toast

4 eggs
1 cup whipping cream   **240 ml**
2 thick slices bread, cut into 3 strips
Powdered sugar

- Place a little oil in skillet. Beat eggs, cream and pinch of salt.
- Dip bread into batter and allow batter to soak in.
- Fry bread in skillet until brown, turn and fry on other side. Transfer to baking sheet. Bake at 325° (162° C) for about 4 minutes or until they puff. Sprinkle with powdered sugar.

Pineapple Slices

1 cup cooked ground ham   **240 ml**
1 teaspoon mustard   **5 ml**
2 tablespoons mayonnaise   **30 ml**
5 slices pineapple, drained

- Combine ham, mustard and mayonnaise and mix well. Spread on pineapple slices.
- Bake in ungreased baking pan at 375° (190° C) for about 15 minutes or until thoroughly hot.

I Love Breakfast At Night

Orange-French Toast

1 egg, beaten	
½ cup orange juice	120 ml
5 slices raisin bread	
1 cup crushed graham crackers	240 ml
2 tablespoons butter	30 ml

- Combine egg and orange juice. Dip each slice of bread in egg mixture and then in graham cracker crumbs.
- Fry in butter until brown.

■

Stained-Glass Fruit Salad

3 bananas, sliced	
1 (16 ounce) package frozen unsweetened strawberries, drained	.5 kg
1 (20 ounce) can pineapple tidbits, drained	567 g
2 (20 ounce) cans peach pie filling	2 (567 g)

- Drain all fruits except peach pie filling. Mix fruits and pie filling together, chill and place in pretty crystal bowl. Refrigerate overnight if possible.

How Many, Kids?

Bacon and Egg Burrito

2 slices bacon, cooked, chopped
2 eggs, scrambled
¼ cup shredded cheddar cheese   60 ml
1 flour tortilla

- Sprinkle bacon, eggs and cheese in middle of tortilla. (Add salsa, if you like.)
- Fold tortilla sides over and place seam-side down on dinner plate. Microwave for 30 seconds or just until it is hot.

■

Peachy Fruit Dip

1 (15 ounce) can sliced peaches, drained   425 g
½ cup marshmallow cream   120 ml
1 (3 ounce) package cream cheese, cubed   84 g
⅛ teaspoon ground nutmeg   .5 ml

- In blender or food processor, combine all ingredients. Serve with assorted fresh fruit.

■ ■ ■

Tortillas All Around

Breakfast Tacos

4 eggs	
4 flour tortillas	
1 cup chopped, cooked ham	**240 ml**
1 cup grated cheddar cheese	**240 ml**

- Scramble eggs in skillet. Lay tortillas flat and spoon eggs over 4 tortillas.
- Sprinkle with ham and cheese and roll to enclose filling.
- Place tacos in microwave-safe dish. Microwave for about 30 seconds or until cheese melts. Serve immediately.

■

Pepper Hot Chocolate

3 cups hot milk, divided	**710 ml**
8 small chocolate peppermint patties	
1 cup half-and-half cream	**240 ml**

- Combine ½ cup (120 ml) hot milk with chocolate peppermint patties in small bowl and stir well. Add pinch of salt and pour into saucepan with remaining hot milk.
- Heat milk to simmering, but do not boil. Add half-and-half cream, stir and serve.

Sunday Night Surprise

Bacon-Cheese Stromboli

1 (10 ounce) tube refrigerated pizza dough	280 g
¾ cup shredded cheddar cheese	180 ml
¾ cup shredded mozzarella cheese	180 ml
6 bacon strips, cooked, crumbled	

- Roll dough into 12-inch (32 cm) circle on ungreased baking sheet. On one-half of dough, sprinkle cheeses and bacon to within ½-inch (1.2 cm) of edge.
- Fold dough over filling and pinch edges to seal. Bake at 400° (204° C) for about 10 minutes or until golden. Serve with salsa. Cut in pie slices.

■

Strawberry Smoothie

2 bananas, peeled, sliced	
1 pint fresh strawberries, washed, quartered	.5 kg
1 (8 ounce) container strawberry yogurt	227 g
¼ cup orange juice	60 ml

- Place all ingredients in blender. Process until smooth.

KIDS-COOK NIGHT

Favorite Twist

Grandkid's Special

Peanut butter
Grape or plum jelly
4 slices white bread, crusts trimmed
2 eggs, well beaten
Butter
Powdered sugar

- Spread peanut butter and jelly on 2 slices of bread. Top with remaining 2 slices of bread. Beat eggs with 2 tablespoons (30 ml) water in shallow bowl. Dip each sandwich in egg.

- Melt about 2 tablespoons (30 ml) butter in skillet and cook each sandwich on both sides until light brown. Take out of skillet and sprinkle lightly with powdered sugar.

■

Franks and Veggie Soup

¼ cup (½ stick) butter	**60 ml**
2 onions, finely chopped	
1 sweet red bell pepper, seeded, chopped	
1 (28 ounce) can baked beans	**794 g**
1 (10 ounce) package frozen mixed vegetables	**280 g**
1 (14 ounce) can beef broth	**396 g**
6 frankfurters, cut into 1-inch slices	**2.5 cm**
1 cup shredded processed cheese	**240 ml**

- Melt butter in large saucepan over medium heat and cook onions and bell pepper for about 5 minutes. Stir in beans, mixed vegetables, broth, frankfurters and 1 cup (240 ml) water. Cook over medium heat, stirring occasionally, until thoroughly hot. Ladle into individual soup bowls and sprinkle each serving with cheese.

I Have It Covered!

No-Fuss Meatballs

1 (14 ounce) package frozen cooked meatballs, thawed	396 g
1 tablespoon soy sauce	15 ml
½ cup chili sauce	120 ml
⅔ cup grape or plum jelly	160 ml
¼ cup dijon-style mustard	60 ml

- In skillet, cook meatballs in soy sauce until it is hot. Combine chili sauce, jelly and mustard and pour over meatballs.
- Cook and stir until jelly dissolves and mixture comes to a boil. Reduce heat, cover and simmer for about 5 minutes.

■

Creamy Dilly Dip

1 (8 ounce) carton sour cream	227 g
1 cup mayonnaise	240 ml
2 tablespoons lemon juice	30 ml
4 green onions with tops, chopped	
1 tablespoon dill weed	15 ml
2 teaspoons white wine Worcestershire sauce	10 ml

- Combine all ingredients until well blended. (Do not use the dark Worcestershire. The white wine Worcestershire keeps this dip light in color and texture.)
- Sprinkle lightly with paprika for color. Cover and refrigerate. Serve with carrot sticks, broccoli flowerets or jicama sticks.

■

Twinkie Dessert

1 (10 count) box Twinkies	
4 bananas, sliced	
1 (5 ounce) package vanilla instant pudding	143 g
1 (20 ounce) can crushed pineapple, drained	567 g
1 (8 ounce) carton whipped topping	227 g

- Slice Twinkies in half lengthwise and place in buttered 9 x 13-inch (23 x 33 cm) pan cream side up. Make layer of sliced bananas.
- Prepare pudding according to package directions (use 2 cups/240 ml milk), pour over bananas and add pineapple. Top with whipped topping and refrigerate. Cut into squares to serve.

Everybody Loves Meatloaf

A Wicked Meatloaf

1 (7 ounce) package stuffing mix plus seasoning packet	198 g
1 egg	
½ cup salsa	120 ml
1½ pounds lean ground beef	680 g

- In bowl combine stuffing mix, seasoning, egg, salsa and ⅓ cup (80 ml) water and mix well. Add ground beef to stuffing mixture.
- Spoon into 9 x 5-inch (23 x 13 cm) loaf pan and bake at 350° (176° C) for 1 hour.

■

Corn Au Gratin

3 (15 ounce) cans mexicorn, drained	3 (425 g)
1 (4 ounce) can sliced mushrooms, drained	114 g
1 (10 ounce) can cream of mushroom soup	280 g
1 cup shredded cheddar cheese	240 ml

- Mix all ingredients in saucepan and heat slowly until cheese melts. Serve hot.

■ ■ ■

Pizza Every Night

Pizza In A Bowl

1 pound lean ground beef	.5 kg
1 (26 ounce) jar marinara or spaghetti sauce	737 g
2 teaspoons dried oregano	10 ml
1 (16 ounce) package shredded mozzarella cheese	.5 kg
¾ teaspoon garlic powder	4 ml

- In saucepan, cook beef over medium heat until no longer pink and drain.
- Stir in marinara sauce and oregano and simmer about 15 minutes. Gradually stir in cheese until it melts.
- Pour into fondue pot or small slow cooker to keep warm. Serve with Italian toast (panetini) found in the deli.

■

Peanut Butter Brownies

1 (20 ounce) package brownie mix	567 g
1 cup peanut butter morsels	240 ml

- Prepare brownie mix according to package directions and stir in peanut butter morsels. Spoon mixture into greased 9 x 13-inch (23 x 33 cm) baking pan.
- Bake at 350° (176° C) for 35 minutes. Cool and cut into squares.

■ ■ ■

You Won't Believe It, But It Works

Baggie Omelet For One

2 eggs	Chopped onions
Shredded cheese	Chopped mushrooms
Chopped bell peppers	Crumbled bacon
Chopped tomatoes	Chopped ham

- Crack eggs in 7-inch (18 cm) plastic bag with zip lock. Choose favorite ingredients and place in baggie. Seal, zip lock and shake to mix ingredients and "scramble" eggs.
- Place in boiling water for 13 minutes. Pick up baggie with tongs and cool for several minutes before opening. Roll omelet out of baggie onto plate and serve.

TIP: *This is no joke. It's so easy*

■

Spiced Pears

1 (15 ounce) can pear halves	425 g
⅓ cup packed brown sugar	80 ml
¾ teaspoon ground nutmeg	4 ml
¾ teaspoon ground cinnamon	4 ml

- Drain pears, reserve syrup and set pears aside.
- Place syrup, brown sugar, nutmeg and cinnamon in saucepan and bring to boil. Reduce heat and simmer uncovered for 5 to 8 minutes, stirring frequently.
- Add pears and simmer for 5 minutes longer or until thoroughly hot.

A Must For Kids

Chili Pie

2 cups small corn chips	480 ml
1 onion, chopped	
1 (19 ounce) can chili without beans	538 g
1½ cups grated cheddar cheese	360 ml

- In 7 x 11-inch (18 x 28 cm) baking dish, place corn chips and top with onion, chili and cheese.
- Bake at 350° (176° C) for about 15 minutes.

■

Swiss Salad

1 large head romaine lettuce	
1 bunch fresh green onions with tops, chopped	
1 (8 ounce) package shredded Swiss cheese	227 g
½ cup sunflower seeds, toasted	120 ml

- Tear lettuce into bite-size pieces. Add onions, cheese, sunflower seeds and toss. Serve with vinaigrette dressing.

TIP: *Toasting brings out the flavors of nuts and seeds. Place nuts on baking sheet and bake at 225° (107° C) for 10 minutes. Be careful not to burn them.*

■

Vinaigrette for Swiss Salad:

⅔ cup salad oil	160 ml
⅓ cup red wine vinegar	80 ml
1 tablespoon seasoned salt	15 ml

- Mix all ingredients and refrigerate.

Always Good To Serve

Chicken Salad

6 - 8 boneless, skinless chicken breast halves	
½ cup chopped celery	120 ml
½ cup chopped onion	120 ml
2 eggs, hard-boiled, diced	
6 tablespoons mayonnaise	90 ml

- In large saucepan boil chicken breast halves in enough water to cover for 30 to 40 minutes.
- Cool, dice chicken and place in large bowl. Add onion, celery, eggs and mayonnaise and mix well. Salt and pepper to taste.
- Spread on favorite bread, mound on lettuce leaves or stuff in hollowed out tomato.

■

Cheese Drops

2 cups baking mix	480 ml
⅔ cup milk	160 ml
⅔ cup grated sharp cheddar cheese	160 ml
¼ cup (½ stick) butter, melted	60 ml

- Mix baking mix, milk and cheese in bowl. Drop 1 heaping tablespoon of dough for each biscuit onto sprayed, baking sheet.
- Bake at 400° (204° C) for 10 minutes or until light brown. While warm, brush tops of biscuits with melted butter. Serve hot.

A "Must-Know" Recipe

Egg Salad

4 eggs, hard-boiled	
⅓ cup mayonnaise	80 ml
1 tablespoon dijon-style mustard	15 ml
1 rib celery, minced	
Bread	

- Mash eggs with fork and stir in mayonnaise, mustard and celery. Add salt and pepper to taste. Spread on bread and serve as sandwiches.

■

Toasted Pepperoni

1 (5 ounce) box melba toasts	143 g
¾ cup chili sauce	180 ml
1 (5 ounce) package pepperoni rounds	143 g
1 cup shredded mozzarella cheese	240 ml

- Spread toast with chili sauce and top with pepperoni slices. Sprinkle with cheese and bake on cookie sheet at 375° (190° C) for 3 to 5 minutes.

■

Easiest Grape Punch

½ gallon ginger ale	2 L
Red seedless grapes	
Sparkling white grape juice, chilled	

- Make ice cubes of ginger ale and seedless grapes. When ready to serve, pour sparkling white grape juice in tall glasses with ginger ale ice cubes.

Basic Survival Food

Tuna Fish Salad

1 (12 ounce) can tuna fish, drained	340 g
½ cup chopped celery	120 ml
¼ cup chopped pecans	60 ml
2 eggs, hard-boiled, finely chopped	
¼ teaspoon onion salt	1 ml
Mayonnaise	

- Drain tuna and put in medium bowl. Add celery, pecans, eggs, onion salt and enough mayonnaise to moisten mixture. Chill and serve.

TIP: *You don't have to use chopped pecans or onion salt to make it good. Some people add seedless, grape halves too.*

■

Corn Sticks

2 cups biscuit mix	480 ml
2 tablespoons minced green onion	30 ml
1 (8 ounce) can cream-style corn	227 g
Butter, melted	

- Mix biscuit mix, green onions and cream-style corn. Place dough on floured surface and cut into 3 x 1-inch (8 x 2.5 cm) strips. Roll in melted butter.
- Bake at 400° (204° C) for 14 to 15 minutes. Dip in melted butter.

Mom's Special

Sweet-and-Sour Glaze for Ham or Wieners

Wonderful sauce to serve with ham slices or sliced wieners to serve with toothpick for appetizers.

> 1 (6 ounce) jar yellow mustard
> 1 (12 ounce) jar grape or plum jelly
> Ham slices or sliced wieners

- In saucepan, combine mustard and jelly and heat, while stirring until mixture is smooth. Serve over ham or wieners.

■

Mom's Mac and Cheese

1 (10 ounce) package favorite macaroni	280 g
¼ cup (½ stick) butter	60 ml
5 tablespoons flour	75 ml
2¾ cups whole milk, divided	660 ml
1 (8 ounce) package shredded cheddar cheese, divided	227 g

- Boil 2 quarts (2 L) water in large saucepan and cook macaroni with a little salt, until it is tender. Drain, but do not rinse and transfer to large mixing bowl.
- In heavy saucepan, melt butter, add flour and whisk to form smooth mixture. Slowly stir in about ¾ cup (180 ml) milk and whisk to avoid lumps.
- On medium heat, add remaining milk, bring to a boil and reduce heat to a gentle simmer. Whisk until sauce is thick and smooth. Add in three-fourths cheese and stir until cheese melts.
- Pour half sauce over drained macaroni and mix well. Add remaining sauce and stir well. Transfer to serving bowl and garnish with remaining cheese.

■ ■ ■

College Survival Food

Cola Chicken

4 - 6 boneless, skinless chicken breast halves	
1 cup ketchup	240 ml
1 cup cola	240 ml
2 tablespoons Worcestershire sauce	30 ml

- Place chicken in 9 x 13-inch (23 x 33 cm) baking dish. Sprinkle with salt and pepper.
- Mix ketchup, cola and Worcestershire and pour over chicken.
- Cover and bake at 350° (176° C) for 50 minutes.

Rice 'N Beans

4 cups cooked rice	1 L
1 (15 ounce) can pinto beans with liquid	425 g
1 cup shredded cheddar cheese	240 ml
3 tablespoons butter, melted	45 ml

- Mix all ingredients in saucepan.
- Cook over low heat until cheese melts. Serve hot.

■ ■ ■

1 Recipe Kids Need To Know

Tuna Noodles

1 (8 ounce) package wide noodles, cooked, drained	227 g
2 (6 ounce) cans white tuna, drained	2 (168 g)
1 (10 ounce) can cream of chicken soup	280 g
¾ cup milk	180 ml
¾ cup chopped black olives	180 ml

- Place half noodles in 2-quart (2 L) buttered casserole.
- In saucepan, combine tuna, soup, milk and olives. Heat just enough to mix well.
- Pour half soup mixture over noodles and repeat layers.
- Cover and bake at 300° (148° C) for 20 minutes.

■

Crunchy Salad

¼ cup sesame seeds	60 ml
½ cup sunflower seeds	120 ml
½ cup slivered almonds	120 ml
1 head red leaf lettuce	

- Toast sesame seeds, sunflower seeds and almonds at 300° (148° C) for about 10 minutes or until light brown.
- Tear lettuce into bite-size pieces and add seed mixture.
- Toss with creamy Italian dressing.

TIP: *Toasting brings out the flavors of nuts and seeds. Place nuts on baking sheet and bake at 225° (107° C) for 10 minutes. Be careful not to burn them.*

Kids Can Do It

Cheese 'N Weiner Crescents

8 large wieners
4 slices American cheese, cut into 6 strips each
1 (8 ounce) can refrigerated crescent dinner rolls   227 g

- Slit wieners to within ½-inch (1.2 cm) of end and insert 3 strips cheese in each slit.
- Separate crescent dough into 8 triangles and wrap dough over wiener keeping cheese side up. Place on cookie sheet.
- Bake at 375° (190° C) for 12 to 15 minutes or until golden brown.

■

Peanut Butter Cookies

1 cup sugar   **240 ml**
¾ cup light corn syrup   **180 ml**
1 (16 ounce) jar crunchy peanut butter   **.5 kg**
4½ cups chow mein noodles   **1.1 L**

- In saucepan over medium heat, bring sugar and corn syrup to boil and stir in peanut butter.
- Remove from heat and stir in noodles.
- Drop by spoonfuls onto waxed paper and allow to cool.

■ ■ ■

This Meal Is Really Easy.

Tangy Pork Chops

4 - 6 pork chops
¼ cup Worcestershire sauce   **60 ml**
¼ cup ketchup   **60 ml**
½ cup honey   **120 ml**

- In skillet, brown pork chop. Place in shallow baking dish.
- Combine Worcestershire, ketchup and honey. Pour over pork chops.
- Cover and bake at 325° (162° C) for 45 minutes.

■

Easy Rice

1 onion, finely chopped
2 tablespoons (¼ stick) butter   **30 ml**
1 cup uncooked white rice   **240 ml**
2 (14 ounce) cans chicken broth   **2 (396 g)**

- Saute onion in butter until transparent.
- In 2-quart (2 L) casserole combine onion, rice and broth. Cover and bake at 350° (176° C) for 55 minutes.

Good Ole Ham

Mustard Ham

1 (1-inch) slice cooked ham	2.5 cm
2 teaspoons dry mustard	10 ml
⅓ cup honey	80 ml
⅓ cup cooking wine	80 ml

- Rub ham slice with 1 teaspoon (5 ml) mustard for each side. Place in shallow baking pan.
- Combine honey and wine and pour over ham.
- Bake uncovered at 350° (176° C) for about 35 minutes.

■

Ranch-Mashed Potatoes

4 cups prepared, unsalted instant mashed potatoes	1 L
1 (1 ounce) package dry ranch-style salad dressing mix	28 g
¼ cup (½ stick) butter	60 ml
½ cup sour cream	120 ml

- Combine all ingredients in saucepan.
- Heat on low until potatoes are hot.

Kids' Soccer Lunch

Pigs In A Blanket

1 (10 count) package wieners
3 (10 count) cans biscuits
Dijon-style mustard

- Cut each wiener into thirds. Flatten each biscuit slightly and spread with mustard. Wrap each wiener piece in biscuit and pinch to seal.
- Bake at 400° (204° C) for 10 to 12 minutes.

■

Peanutty Grahams

1 (8 ounce) package cream cheese, softened	**227 g**
1¾ cups creamy peanut butter	**420 ml**
¾ cup powdered white sugar	**180 ml**
1 tablespoon milk	**15 ml**
1 box graham crackers	

- With mixer, beat cream cheese, peanut butter, sugar and milk. Spread on graham crackers.

It's My Turn, Mom.

Speedy Cheese Dip

2 (10 ounce) cans cheddar cheese soup	2 (280 g)
1 (10 ounce) can diced tomatoes and green chilies	280 g
1 (10 ounce) can cream of chicken soup	280 g
Pinch cayenne pepper	

- Mix all ingredients in saucepan. Add ½ teaspoon (2 ml) salt to taste. Serve hot. Serve with chips.

■

Chalupas

12 flat, crispy corn tortillas	
1 (15 ounce) can refried beans	425 g
1 (12 ounce) package shredded cheddar cheese	340 g
1 cup chopped lettuce	240 ml
2 tomatoes, chopped	
1 large onion, chopped	
Salsa	

- Preheat oven to 300° (148 C). Separate tortillas, spread refried beans over each tortilla and sprinkle cheese on top.
- Place on baking sheets and heat just until cheese melts. Remove from oven and top with lettuce, tomato, onion and salsa. Serve immediately.

TIP: *If you cannot find the crispy, flat tortillas, buy the soft ones and fry in hot oil until they are crispy. Drain thoroughly, top with refried beans, cheese, lettuce, tomato, onion and salsa and serve immediately.*

EDITORS CHOICE

Southern Macaroni and Cheese

1 (16 ounce) package shell pasta	.5 kg
2 tablespoons (¼ stick) butter	30 ml
3 eggs, beaten	
1 (16 ounce) carton half-and-half cream	.5 kg
1 (12 ounce) package cheddar cheese, divided	340 g
⅛ teaspoon cayenne pepper	.5 ml

- Preheat oven to 350°. Combine pasta and 2 teaspoons (10 ml) salt in large saucepan and cook for 6 minutes. (Pasta should not be cooked completely.)
- Drain pasta and stir in butter to keep it from sticking. Transfer to sprayed 2½-quart (2.5 L) baking dish.
- In bowl, combine eggs, cream, three-fourths cheese and cayenne pepper and mix well. Pour mixture over pasta and sprinkle remaining cheese over top.
- Cover and bake for 35 minutes. Remove cover and broil just enough to lightly brown top.

■

Pink Lemonade Pie

1 (6 ounce) can pink lemonade frozen concentrate	168 g
1 (14 ounce) can sweetened condensed milk	396 g
1 (12 ounce) package whipped topping	340 g
1 (6 ounce) graham cracker piecrust	168 g

- Combine lemonade concentrate and condensed milk in large bowl and blend well. Fold in whipped topping and pour into piecrust. Refrigerate overnight.

Oh Happy Night

Loaded Baked Potatoes

6 medium potatoes	
1 (1 pound) hot sausage	.5 kg
2 (16 ounce) packages cubed processed cheese	2 (.5 kg)
1 (10 ounce) can tomatoes and green chilies	280 g

- Wrap potatoes in foil and bake at 375°(190° C) for 1 hour or until done.
- Brown sausage and drain. Add cubed cheese to sausage. Heat until cheese melts and add tomatoes and green chilies.
- Serve sausage-cheese mixture over baked potatoes.

■

Merry Berry Salad

1 (10 ounce) package mixed salad greens	280 g
1 red and 1 green apple with peels, diced	
1 cup shredded parmesan cheese	240 ml
½ cup sweetened dried cranberries or craisins	120 ml
½ cup slivered almonds, toasted	120 ml
Poppy seed dressing	

- In large salad bowl, toss greens, apples, cheese, cranberries and almonds. Drizzle prepared poppy seed dressing over salad and toss.

TIP: *Toasting brings out the flavors of nuts and seeds. Place nuts on baking sheet and bake at 225° (107° C) for 10 minutes. Be careful not to burn them.*

Couch Potatoes and Cookies

Broccoli-Topped Potatoes

4 hot baked potatoes, halved	
1 cup diced cooked ham	240 ml
1 (10 ounce) can cream of broccoli soup	280 g
½ cup shredded cheddar cheese	120 ml

- Place hot baked potatoes on microwave-safe plate. Carefully fluff up potatoes with fork. Top each potato with ham.
- Stir soup in can until smooth. Spoon soup over potatoes and top with cheese. Microwave on high for 4 minutes.

■

New Orleans Praline Shortbreads

1 cup (½ stick) butter, softened	240 ml
¾ cup packed light brown sugar	180 ml
1½ cups flour	360 ml
¾ cup chopped pecans	180 ml

- Combine butter and brown sugar with mixer until ingredients are light and fluffy. Stir in flour and pecans and mix well.
- Spray 9 x 13-inch (23 x 33 cm) baking pan and sprinkle with flour. Spread dough in pan evenly and bake at 325° (162° C) for about 20 minutes or until light brown. Cut into squares and serve.

Oh Boy!

Banana Split Sunday

You don't always have to have real food on Sunday nights. That's what makes it memorable.

1 firm banana	
1 scoop each: vanilla, chocolate, strawberry ice cream	
2 tablespoons each: chocolate syrup, strawberry syrup, butterscotch sauce	30 ml
Whipped cream	
Maraschino cherries	
2 tablespoons chopped nuts	30 ml

- Peel banana and slice in 2 pieces lengthwise. Put 1 scoop each of vanilla, chocolate and strawberry ice cream between slices of banana.
- Pour chocolate syrup, strawberry syrup and butterscotch sauce over scoops of ice cream.
- Top with whipped cream, maraschino cherries and nuts.

■ ■ ■

Sundaes For Sunday

Hot Fudge Sundae

1 cup semi-sweet chocolate chips	240 ml
1 tablespoon butter	15 ml
¼ cup sugar	60 ml
½ cup evaporated milk	120 ml
Vanilla ice cream	
Chopped nuts	
Whipped topping	
Maraschino cherries	

- In heavy saucepan over low heat, melt chocolate, butter and sugar, stirring constantly. Remove from heat, pour in milk and stir until smooth.
- In separate bowl, place 1 or 2 scoops vanilla ice cream, pour hot fudge over top, sprinkle nuts, whipped topping and maraschino cherry on top. Serve immediately.

Peanut Butter Sundae

1 cup light corn syrup	240 ml
1 cup chunky peanut butter	240 ml
¼ cup milk	60 ml
Ice cream	

- Stir together corn syrup, peanut butter and milk in mixing bowl until they blend well. Serve over ice cream and store in refrigerator.

Pizza Tips

Pizza holds a lofty position in American society in that it's quick, it's easy, it's accessible and it can be created to please everyone in the group. Whether it's adding a topping or deleting another, there are many ways to add variety and flavor to pizza thereby making an "old stand-by" something special. It's also an easy way to involve the kids in dinner preparations, and it's fun in the process! The following toppings are some ideas to add a little pizzazz to your next pizza creation!

1.   Black Olives
2.   Sun-Dried Tomatoes
3.   Pesto (Can get readily prepared at most grocery stores)
4.   Grated Romano
5.   Grated Parmesan
6.   Ricotta Cheese
7.   Garlic Powder
8.   Italian Seasoning
9.   Canned Tuna
10.   Shrimp
11.   White Pizza — Alfredo Sauce & Spinach
12.   Taco Pizza — Taco Seasoning, Hamburger Meat, Cheddar Cheese, and add lettuce after pizza has cooled
13.   Drizzled Olive Oil
14.   Ham & Pineapple
15.   Salami
16.   Cabicolla
17.   Grilled Chicken

U.S. Measurements & Food Equivalents

3 teaspoons	1 tablespoon	
4 tablespoons	¼ cup	2 fluid ounces
8 tablespoons	½ cup	4 fluid ounces
12 tablespoons	¾ cup	6 fluid ounces
16 tablespoons	1 cup	8 fluid ounces
¼ cup	4 tablespoons	2 fluid ounces
⅓ cup	5 tablespoons + 1 teaspoons	
½ cup	8 tablespoons	4 fluid ounces
⅔ cup	10 tablespoons + 2 teaspoons	
¾ cup	12 tablespoons	6 fluid ounces
1 cup	16 tablespoons	8 fluid ounces
1 cup	½ pint	
2 cups	1 pint	16 fluid ounces
3 cups	1½ pints	24 fluid ounces
4 cups	1 quart	32 fluid ounces
8 cups	2 quarts	64 fluid ounces
1 pint	2 cups	16 fluid ounces
2 pints	1 quart	
1 quart	2 pints; 4 cups	32 fluid ounces
4 quarts	1 gallon; 8 pints; 16 cups	
8 quarts	1 peck	

Cake Pans

5 x 2 round	2⅔ cups
6 x 2 round	3¾ cups
8 x 1.5 round	4 cups
7 x 2 round	5¼ cups
8 x 2 round	6 cups
9 x 1.5 round	6 cups
9 x 2 round	8 cups
9 x 3 bundt	9 cups
10 x 3.5 bundt	12 cups
9.5 x 2.5 springform	10 cups
10 x 2.5 springform	12 cups
8 x 3 tube	9 cups
9 x 4 tube	11 cups
10 x 4 tube	16 cups

Casseroles

8 x 8 x12 square	8 cups
11 x7 x 12 rectangular	8 cups
9 x9 x 2 square	10 cups
13 x 9 x 2 rectangular	15 cups
1-quart casserole	4 cups
2-quart casserole	8 cups
2.5 quart casserole	10 cups
3-quart casserole	12 cups

Ingredient Equivalents

Food	Amount	Approximate Equivalent
Apples	1 pound fresh	3 medium; 2¼ cups chopped; 3 cups sliced
Bacon	1 slice, cooked	1 tablespoons crumbled
Bread	1 (1 pound) loaf	14 - 18 regular slices; 7 cups crumbs
	1 slice	½ cup crumbs
Breadcrumbs	1 (8 ounce) package	2⅓ cups
Breadcrumbs, dry	1 cup	¾ cup cracker crumbs
Broccoli	1 pound fresh	2 cups chopped
Broth, chicken or beef	1 cup	1 bouillon cube; 1 teaspoon granules in 1 cup boiling water
Butter	1 pound regular	4 sticks; 2 cups;
	1 stick	½ cup; 8 tablespoons
	1 cup (4 ounces)	⅞ cup vegetable oil or Shortening; 1 cup margarine
Buttermilk	1 cup	1 tablespoon lemon juice or white vinegar plus milk to equal 1 cup (must stand for 5 minutes)
Celery	2 ribs	½ cup chopped
Cottage Cheese	1 cup	1 cup ricotta
Crackers	15 graham crackers	1 cup crumbs
	28 saltine crackers	1 cup crumbs
Cream	½ pint light	1 cup
	½ pint whipping	1 cup; 2 cups whipped
	½ pint sour cream	1 cup
Cream Cheese	8 ounces	1 cup
Chicken	3 - 3½ pounds	3 cups cooked meat
	1 whole breast	1½ cups cooked, chopped
Chocolate	6 ounce chips	1 cup
Chocolate wafers	18 - 20 cookies	1 cup crumbs
Cornstarch	1 tablespoon	2 tablespoons flour
Cream, whipping	1 cup	4 ounces frozen whipped topping
Flour	1 cup sifted all-purpose	1 cup minus 2 tablespoons unsifted all-purpose
	1 cup sifted self-rising	1 cup sifted all-purpose flour plus 1½ teaspoons baking powder plus ⅛ teaspoon salt
Garlic	1 small clove	⅛ teaspoon garlic powder
Grits	1 pound	3 cups
Ham	½ pound boneless	1½ cups chopped
Herbs	1 tablespoon fresh	1 teaspoon dried
Honey	1 cup	1¼ cups granulated sugar plus ⅓ cup liquid in recipe
Ketchup	½ cup	½ cup tomato sauce plus 2 tablespoons sugar plus 1 tablespoon vinegar
Lemon juice	1 teaspoon	½ teaspoon vinegar
Lemons	4 - 6	1 cup juice
Limes	6 - 8	¾ cup juice
Macaroni	8 ounces	4 cups cooked
	1 cup	1¾ cups cooked
Marshmallows	6 - 7 large	1 cup
	85 miniature	1 cup
Milk	1 quart	4 cups

Ingredient Equivalents

Food	Amount	Approximate Equivalent
Milk, evaporated	5 ounce can	⅔ cup
Mushrooms	½ pound fresh	1 (6 ounce) can, drained
	1 pound	5 cups sliced; 6 cups chopped
Mustard	1 tablespoon prepared	1 teaspoon dry
Oil	1 quart	4 cups
Onions	1 small	1 tablespoon instant minced; ½ tablespoon onion powder
Onions, green	5 bulbs only	½ cup chopped
	5 with tops	1¾ cups chopped
Onions, white	4 medium	3½ cups chopped
Oreo	22 cookies	1½ cups crumbs
Peaches	4 medium	2½ cups chopped or sliced
Peanut Butter	18 ounce jar	1¾ cups
Pecans	1 pound shelled	4 cups chopped
Peppers, bell	2 large	2½ cups chopped; 3 cups sliced
	1 medium	1 cup chopped
Potatoes, sweet	3 medium	4 cups chopped
Potatoes, white, red, russet	1 pound	4 cups chopped
Rice	1 cup regular	3 cups cooked
	1 cup instant	2 cups cooked
	1 cup brown	4 cups cooked
	1 cup wild	4 cups cooked
Shortening	1 pound	2½ cups
Shrimp	1 pound shelled	2 cups cooked
	1 pound in shell	20 - 30 large; 11 - 15 jumbo
Sour cream	1 cup	1 cup plain yogurt; ¾ cup buttermilk; 1 tablespoon lemon juice plus enough evaporated milk to equal 1 cup
Squash	1 pound summer	3 cups sliced
	1 pound winter	1 cup cooked, mashed
Strawberries	1 pint fresh	1½ cups sliced
	10 ounces frozen	1½ cups
Sugar	1 cup light brown	½ cup packed brown sugar plus ½ cup granulated sugar
	1 cup granulated	1¾ cups confections sugar; 1 cup packed brown sugar; 1 cup superfine sugar
	1 pound granulated	2 cups
	1 pound confectioners	3½ cups
	1 pound brown	2¼ cups packed
Tomatoes	3 medium	1½ cups chopped
Tomato juice	1 cup	½ cup tomato paste plus ½ cup water
Tomato sauce	1 cup	½ cup tomato paste plus ½ cup water
Vanilla wafers	22 cookies	1 cup crumbs
Wine	750 ml	3 cups
Yogurt	1 cup	1 cup buttermilk; 1 cup plus 1 tablespoon lemon juice

Master Grocery List

Fresh Produce

___ Apples
___ Avocados
___ Bananas
___ Beans
___ Bell Peppers
___ Broccoli
___ Cabbage
___ Carrots
___ Cauliflower
___ Celery
___ Corn
___ Cucumbers
___ Garlic
___ Grapefruit
___ Grapes
___ Lemons
___ Lettuce
___ Lime
___ Melons
___ Mushrooms
___ Onions
___ Oranges
___ Peaches
___ Pears
___ Peppers
___ Potatoes
___ Strawberries
___ Spinach
___ Squash
___ Tomatoes
___ Zucchini
___ _____
___ _____

Deli

___ Cheese
___ Chicken
___ Main Dish
___ Prepared Salad
___ Sandwich Meat
___ Side Dishes
___ _____
___ _____

Fresh Bakery

___ Bagels
___ Bread
___ Cake
___ Cookies
___ Croissants
___ Donuts
___ French Bread
___ Muffins
___ Pastries
___ Pies
___ Rolls

Dairy

___ Biscuits
___ Butter
___ Cheese
___ Cottage Cheese
___ Cream Cheese
___ Cream
___ Creamer
___ Eggs
___ Juice
___ Margarine
___ Milk
___ Pudding
___ Sour Cream
___ Yogurt
___ _____
___ _____

Frozen Foods

___ Breakfast
___ Dinners
___ Ice
___ Ice Cream
___ Juice
___ Pastries
___ Pies
___ Pizza
___ Potatoes
___ Vegetables
___ Whipped Cream
___ _____
___ _____

Grocery

___ Beans
___ Beer/Wine
___ Bread
___ Canned Vegetables
___ _____
___ _____
___ Cereal
___ Chips/Snacks
___ Coffee
___ Cookies
___ Crackers
___ Flour
___ Honey
___ Jelly
___ Juice
___ Ketchup
___ Kool-Aid
___ Mayonnaise
___ Mixes
___ _____
___ _____
___ Mustard
___ Nuts/Seeds
___ Oil
___ Pasta
___ Peanut Butter
___ Pickles/Olives
___ Popcorn
___ Rice
___ Salad Dressing
___ Salt

Grocery (continued)

___ Seasonings
___ _____
___ _____
___ Sauce
___ Sodas
___ Soups
___ Spices
___ _____
___ _____
___ Sugar
___ Syrup
___ Tea
___ Tortillas
___ Water
___ _____
___ _____

Meat

___ Bacon
___ Chicken
___ Ground Beef
___ Ham
___ Hot Dogs
___ Pork
___ Roast
___ Sandwich Meat
___ Sausage
___ Steak
___ Turkey
___ _____
___ _____

General Merchandise

___ Automotive
___ Baby Items
___ _____
___ Bath Soap
___ Bath Tissue
___ Deodorant
___ Detergent
___ Dish Soap
___ Facial Tissue
___ Feminine Products
___ Aluminum Foil
___ Greeting Cards
___ Hardware
___ Insecticides
___ Light Bulbs
___ Lotion
___ Medicine
___ Napkins
___ Paper Plates
___ Paper Towels
___ Pet Supplies
___ Prescriptions
___ Shampoo
___ Toothpaste
___ Vitamins
___ _____
___ _____

Thank you for your patronage.

Bringing Family and Friends To The Table

cookbook resources LLC

866-229-2665
www.cookbookresources.com

Index

Sunday Night Suppers

Recipe Names & Categories

Index

Index

Index

Index

Index

Index

Chicken & Turkey

Index

Chocolate

Index

Index

Index

Index

Index

Index

N

Nuts

Index

Index

Index

Index

S

Salads

Index

Index

Index

Index

Notes:

Notes:

Notes:

Featured Cookbooks

The Best 1001 Short, Easy Recipes is the
best cookbook for easy recipes and easy meals every family will
love. Recipes are 5 ingredients or less and use ingredients right
from your pantry. These short, easy recipes are lifesavers for
cooks who want to spend less time in the kitchen and more time
around the table with the family.
    Try these favorites:
Quick Adobe Chicken
Turkey-Asparagus Sandwiches
Chocolate Kisses
$19.95 free shipping   Hard cover with lay-flat binding

Easy Slow Cooking just makes life easier! These
recipes are so easy anyone can cook them and they are so
delicious everyone will love them.
    Don't miss:
Roasted Red Pepper pork Tenderloin
Cajun Bean Soup
Bacon-Wrapped Chicken
Chocolate Fondue

$19.95 free shipping   Hard cover with lay-flat binding

Quick Fixes With Cake Mixes shows you how
to add a few extra ingredients to cake mixes for that made-from-
scratch taste. Simple cakes you can serve from the pan and
special cookies, bars, pies and crunches make this an essential
part of your cookbook library.
    Try these winners:
Caramel-Ribbon Pear Cake
Chocolate-Dipped Malted Milk Cookies
Pecan Pie Bars
$19.95 free shipping   Hard cover with lay-flat binding

Recipe Keeper is your own special recipe collection with
room for more than 1,000 of your favorite recipes and an index
for 100 of your favorite cookbook titles. 12 pockets are great for
clippings, magazine cut-outs and recipe cards. **Recipe Keeper**
makes saving recipes easy.
$19.95 free shipping   Hard cover with lay-flat binding

COOKBOOKS PUBLISHED BY
COOKBOOK RESOURCES, LLC

The Ultimate Cooking with 4 Ingredients
Easy Cooking with 5 Ingredients
The Best of Cooking with 3 Ingredients
Gourmet Cooking with 5 Ingredients
Healthy Cooking with 4 Ingredients
Diabetic Cooking with 4 Ingredients
4-Ingredient Recipes for 30-Minute Meals
Essential 3-4-5 Ingredient Recipes
The Best 1001 Short, Easy Recipes
Easy Slow Cooker Cookbook
Easy One-Dish Meals
Easy Potluck Recipes
Quick Fixes with Cake Mixes
Casseroles to the Rescue
Easy Casseroles
Italian Family Cookbook
Sunday Nigh Suppers
365 Easy Meals
365 Easy Chicken
365 Soups and Stews
I Ain't On No Diet Cookbook
Kitchen Keepsakes/More Kitchen Keepsakes
Old-Fashioned Cookies
Grandmother's Cookies
Mother's Recipes
Recipe Keeper
Cookie Dough Secrets
Gifts for the Cookie Jar
All New Gifts for the Cookie Jar
Gifts in a Pickle Jar
Muffins In A Jar
Brownies In A Jar
Cookie Jar Magic
Easy Desserts
Bake Sale Bestsellers
Quilters' Cooking Companion
Miss Sadie's Southern Cooking
Southern Family Favorites
Classic Tex-Mex and Texas Cooking
Classic Southwest Cooking
The Great Canadian Cookbook
The Best of Lone Star Legacy Cookbook
Cookbook 25 Years
Pass the Plate
Texas Longhorn Cookbook
Trophy Hunters' Wild Game Cookbook
Mealtimes and Memories
Holiday Recipes
Little Taste of Texas
Little Taste of Texas II
Southwest Sizzler
Southwest Olé
Class Treats
Leaving Home

cookbook
resources LLC
Bringing Families To The Table

To Order: *Sunday Night Suppers*

Please send_____ copies @ $16.95 (U.S.) each $ _____

Texas residents add sales tax @ $1.35 each $ _____

Plus postage/handling @ $6.00 (1st copy) $ _____

$1.00 (each additional copy) $ _____

Check or Credit Card (Canada-credit card only) **Total** $ _____

Charge to:

_____ MasterCard   _____ Visa

Account # _____

Expiration Date _____

Signature _____

Mail or Call:
Cookbook Resources
541 Doubletree Drive
Highland Village, Texas 75077
Toll Free (866) 229-2665
Fax (972) 317-6404

Name _____

Address _____

City _____ State _____ Zip _____

Telephone (Day) _____ (Evening) _____

- -

To Order: *Sunday Night Suppers*

Please send_____ copies @ $16.95 (U.S.) each $ _____

Texas residents add sales tax @ $1.35 each $ _____

Plus postage/handling @ $6.00 (1st copy) $ _____

$1.00 (each additional copy) $ _____

Check or Credit Card (Canada-credit card only) **Total** $ _____

Charge to:

_____ MasterCard   _____ Visa

Account # _____

Expiration Date _____

Signature _____

Mail or Call:
Cookbook Resources
541 Doubletree Drive
Highland Village, Texas 75077
Toll Free (866) 229-2665
Fax (972) 317-6404

Name _____

Address _____

City _____ State _____ Zip _____

Telephone (Day) _____ (Evening) _____